MW01118108

TOTAL WELLNESS

A Millennial & Gen Z Guide to Living a More Balanced Life

Also by Rikimah Glymph:

Real Talk: A Book of Love Notes for Black & Brown Womxn

TOTAL WELLNESS

A Millennial & Gen Z Guide to Living a More Balanced Life

RIKIMAH GLYMPH

GLYMPH CONSULTING, LLC

Total Wellness: A Millennial & Gen Z Guide to Living A More Balanced Life

Published by Glymph Consulting, LLC

Copyright © 2022 by Rikimah Glymph
All rights reserved. Neither this book, nor any parts within it may be sold or reproduced in any form or by any electronic or mechanical means, including information storage and retrieval systems, without permission in writing from the author. The only exception is by a reviewer, who may quote short excerpts in a review.

Library of Congress Control Number: 2022937577

Copyright for the image: iStockphoto.com/Kateryna Ovcharenko (abstract design)

ISBN (hardcover): 9781662928291
ISBN (paperback): 9781662928307
eISBN: 9781662928314

| For Millennials and Gen Z. You got this. Keep working at it and know that as long as you never stop trying, you'll always get closer to where you need to be—balanced and well. To my son, Mahlieke, nieces, nephews, brothers, and sisters—your wellness matters. Protect it. Work at it. And never give up. <3 |

Table of Contents

INTRODUCTION

The Generational Wellness Gap

Do you remember when your parents were a much younger version of themselves? Do you recall how agile they were? They might have appeared healthier, happier, and in many instances, more outgoing even though health care was less sophisticated at the time.

What about millennials (this is my generation, a generation of people born between 1977 and 1996)? Do you remember a time when there were no smartphones or social media? A time when we played outside until the streetlights came on, chased ice cream trucks down the streets, went to one cookout after another, and held long conversations with each other about everything and nothing?

As we got older, those days slowly changed and, for some, crept away entirely, filling us with cheerful memories of smiles and wholesome hearts. For others, like myself, the changing times also represented an upgrade from what some might call a traumatic start. Now, born between 1996 and 2012, Generation Z struggles with being able to imagine what those experiences must have felt like. The majority of this generation identifies as socially awkward. Many have difficulties engaging in a worthwhile conversation and, as a result, are more likely to feel lonelier for that reason. This young(er) generation faces a big challenge brought about by access to overwhelming amounts of information, personalized technologies, and social media. Interestingly, the younger generation is the majority, making up 32 percent of the world's population, according to data provided by the United Nations.[1] Millennials make up slightly less, averaging 31.5 percent of the global population.

WHY DOES THIS MATTER?

This matters because millennials make up the majority of the global workforce. Millennials are the only generation in which every member is a working-age adult. According to the Pew Research Center, we (millennials) took the lead in the working population far back in 2016.[2] However, a report by the Blue Cross Blue Shield Association (BCBS) revealed that millennials are in worse health conditions than the preceding Generation X used to be at a similar age.[3] Does this mean that millennials are aging faster than their parents did? Of course not. It simply means that, while we are investing heavily in wellness practices like yoga and meditation, we are unknowingly, or in some cases, knowingly ignoring the other things that matter when it comes to attaining complete wellness.

WHY IS THIS SO CONCERNING?

Throughout my career, I've met with many adults that are constantly swamped with work and overwhelmed with life.

A lot of people are struggling to stay afloat, but only a few are staying above water. Unfortunately, many people are sinking. The rates of depression and suicide among young people around the world are at all-time highs.[4] In the United States and other developed countries where technological advancements are accessible and are supposed to make life easier, the reality is even uglier than you might imagine.

While working for a US-based organization, it didn't take long for me to acknowledge that, contrary to how they were feeling at that moment, staff could in fact be happier and more content overall. They were not finding self-fulfillment in the jobs that they were in, and their productivity was taking a big hit as a result. They weren't the only people affected in this case, though. The organization and managers were affected too. Paying salaries and trying to manage a team of staffers that weren't happy within themselves was, at best, exhausting. Some staffers felt the urge to resign. To leave and try working elsewhere, not minding the potential for pay cuts usually associated with changing jobs and careers. Yes, many considered a change of career.

Interestingly, the reality that usually escapes our minds is simple: Self-fulfillment comes from within. Not through career changes, bonuses, extended vacation, additional paid leave, increased benefits at work, salary raises, or any of the benefits that good organizations offer their employees. Self-fulfillment does not come from material possessions either. Although these perks in our work lives have motivational impacts, they are not the actual drivers of happiness and self-fulfillment. The real drivers are buried deep within.

Over the years, I've wondered if staff members knew this truth. It's possible they did know, but forgot. Or perhaps they didn't forget but had challenges in finding those drivers of self-fulfillment inside of them. It takes self-awareness to realize that you are stretching toward the breaking point. Having this awareness of self and the necessary coping skills to get through difficult times in one piece is critical to our survival. Knowing this, I felt and continue to feel obligated to share what I've gathered to extend a helping hand. To assist staff members in the little ways that I can. Needless to say, it's been exciting to see desired results materialize and staffers improving in their work.

Another reality is that billions of young people around the world are facing similar (or the same) issues that my colleagues faced. It's happening in almost every area of their adult lives, including family, work, social relationships, finance, etc. You may know one of these people. Maybe you are one. Regardless, what's important here is that it's something that you can get out of.

Like all other humans that have existed before me, that are living with me now, and that will grace the earth after I'm long gone, my abilities are finite. I realized early on that I wasn't going to be able to work at every organization out there. While I want to help everyone, the truth is that I'm only one person and, thus, need to find ways to help many at the same time. I know that I may not be able to help everyone going through a hard time to attain total wellness in person. However, the knowledge that I've acquired all these years, and the practical approaches to gaining better control over physical, mental, financial, and social wellness that I shared with my colleagues, are explained in granular detail in this book, and I hope that you find it helpful too.

▌ WHY ARE YOU READING THIS BOOK?

More often than not, many of us are seeking solutions to life's seemingly unending challenges. In doing so, there are two types of people that exist. One type includes those that would be willing to walk the length of the earth in search of solutions to their problems. Others are more proactive. They take preventive measures to ensure that those problems don't occur in the first place. Either way, none of us can be careful enough to avoid life's curveballs in everything that we do. The same applies to our pursuit of wellness.

You may find yourself in a ditch of unwellness and clawing your way out. You might be the person whose life seems to be in perfect order and be quite well-off financially, emotionally, mentally, and physically. Even more, your life condition may be all right, but you may find yourself slipping into a ditch, with several episodes of anxiety and moments of depression. If you identify with the first or third person, clawing your way out of the swamp, you may be looking for ways to improve your state of well-being. Thus, you are reading this book. On the other hand, if you are doing well for yourself, you may be concerned and thinking about how to prevent your wellness from slipping through the cracks. Regardless of what category you find yourself in, this book is written for you. It was written to bring you closer to the knowledge of what complete wellness really means.

WHO IS THIS BOOK FOR?

I wrote this book with a deep concern for millennials and Generation Zers, many of whom are struggling to find balance in life in this rapidly changing world. It seems to me that we're all experiencing some level of overwhelm, and from where I sit, it seems like it's being elevated by the shrinking gap between work and life, parenting and adulting, and socialization and prospecting our future goals or life purpose.

Regardless of our gender representation, we face similar wellness challenges, and so, keeping that in mind, my aim is to help everyone find their unique balance. I urge you to read this book to the end and draw inspiration from it in ways that can help you attain total wellness.

The younger generation, Alpha, is not left out. I believe that the expectations that we have placed on them are higher than those placed on us by preceding generations. This can and will negatively affect their state of well-being. They, as well, need all the background knowledge about wellness that they can get to help them prepare for the bright but unpredictable future ahead of them.

WHAT'S TO COME?

I've divided this book into three parts for easy understanding and flow. In the first part, Understanding Wellness, you will get the opportunity to familiarize yourself with what wellness really means and how it impacts your life on the micro and macro scale.

In the first chapter of this book, The Wellness You Never Knew, I debunk several wellness myths and explain the concept of complete wellness at its granular level. Within those pages, you will gain the basic knowledge of wellness with which you can take practical steps toward improving your own state of well-being. The second chapter, The 8 Pillars of Wellness, explains the different foundations upon which your complete wellness rests.

These pillars are like the four tires of your car. With one in bad shape, you may forfeit the ability to go far without wobbling or even crashing. In worse cases, you may be totally incapacitated and unable to move an inch. The third chapter, The Wellness Wheel, helps tie the concept of all the pillars together to form an interesting wellness cycle. This chapter will help you understand how neglecting one pillar can negatively affect other pillars and, if not addressed soon enough, impact your entire well-being.

The next two chapters make up another part: the second of all three parts, Attaining Total Wellness. Here, you will join me on a practical journey toward achieving a wholesome personality. One with a genuinely cheerful smile and trouble-free soul. This section shows you how to retrace your steps in an effort to become that joy-filled person that made snowballs and socialized with others. The epitome of blessing and happiness that finds self-fulfillment in the things that you do.

In the first chapter of this second part, Sharing the Chores, you will start to understand how challenging it is for many to prioritize wellness across all critical areas. You will learn about your personal responsibilities and those of the people around you on your journey toward total wellness. I will highlight the roles of everyone around you in helping you become whole and will lay out how you can build your expectations accordingly. The succeeding chapter, 5 Steps to Complete Wellness, is a step-by-step guide to help you turn your life around. In the fifth chapter, I connect all that was discussed in the previous chapters. I highlight the understanding that you will have acquired from the first part of the book and anchor it into a practical guide that you can reproduce, share with your loved ones, and implement to build yourself into a self-fulfilled person, as well as those around you.

I believe that life doesn't end with us. We are called to serve and prepare a way for those that will come after us. The third and final part of this book, Extending the Goodness, is focused on this principle. As a parent, I've seen firsthand the need to help younger generations, Generations Z and Alpha (those born in 2013), build a solid wellness foundation. So, the leading chapter, Parental Wellness, is written as a practical guide to help you step more into your parenting as you consider what might help your kids and other children around you. It should go without saying, but their emotions are fragile, and without full self-consciousness, you may unintentionally hurt them, so keeping their wellness at the forefront matters.

The last chapter, Career Wellness, is more organization-oriented. With millennials holding the lion's share of the workforce and Generation Z slowly taking the reins, we all need to maintain our balance in the workplace and build a culture where we are all doing the work that we love in ways that we love.

BEFORE WE BEGIN

It would be uncharitable of me to jump right into this book without first letting you know that you will uncover some challenges on your quest to complete wellness. As you already may know, nothing good comes easy. Nothing is impossible once you set your mind to it, but this journey will require work, sweat, honesty, and rigor. Building wellness requires consistency, specificity, and clarity of goal. You have to be true to yourself because only you can hold yourself accountable to where you are lagging.

As someone that will always be rooting for you and those that you love, I can only cheer you onward to pursue greatness. To be the champion that you want to be. To be well, happy, and fulfilled. Sound in mind and body. Socially buoyant and spiritually agile. To recognize your emotions and hone them as the vital part of you that they are. And, most of all, to find a balance for all your pillars of wellness.

As you flip through the pages of this book, I hope that you find answers to your questions as well as the inspiration to steer your life in the right direction toward wholesomeness.

With tenderheartedness that runs deep,

Rikimah Glymph

PART ONE

Understanding Wellness

CHAPTER ONE

The Wellness You Never Knew

In 1979, a group of German scientists and doctors led by Dr. H. Frisch discovered that our state of mind can affect our ability to grow.[1] They observed that a nine-year-old was suffering from dwarfism and underdevelopment of the bones because the growth hormone and other pituitary hormones were not in sufficient production. If you google the reason for poor production of these hormones, you will find several reasons. These doctors discovered that none of the suspected causes led to dwarfism in this child. By simply changing the child's environment, they noticed a rapid increase in the production of the growth hormone in the child.

Five years later, in 1984, Dr. Frisch, along with other researchers, made another startling discovery. In their case report, they explained that our biological growth as humans is hindered by "emotional deprivations" and the quality of our social environment.[2] This deprivation could cause "delayed intellectual development, abnormal eating and drinking habits and aggressiveness."

These were novel findings in the seventies and eighties. Today, it's our new reality. Many young people are experiencing growth disorders in their emotional, physical, mental, spiritual, and/or financial lives. For some, the challenge is evident in more than one area. And while we struggle to improve our situation, we often find ourselves stuck in a downward spiral. Many are fighting to escape the hollowness that they feel inside. Some others are trying to fill it up. How do I know?

> Wellness is the daily practice of healthy habits to promote better physical, mental, financial, and professional health.

The global wellness economy has experienced twice as much growth as the world economy. According to the Global Wellness Institute, the global wellness market was worth $4.2 trillion in 2020.[3]

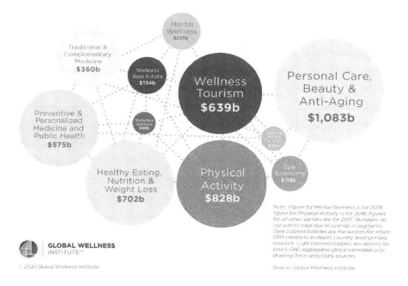

GLOBAL WELLNESS ECONOMY:
$4.5 Trillion Market

The massive size of this market and the enormous growth that it has experienced in the last decade are a clear indication that millennials and Gen Zers are actively seeking out ways to maintain wellness. It turns out, however, that despite this strong commitment, many people are not getting the results that they are paying for. Why? Why do we crave complete wellness, yet the feelings we harbor within us are grossly unsettling? Why are we not getting the results that we've hoped and paid for? Why do many people feel stuck in this downward spiral of unfulfillment?

This chapter is focused on helping you define wellness clearly. At the end, you will be able to identify what wellness is and what it's not, as well as how abstract factors play a role in helping you attain wellness.

OUR REALITY IS SHAPED FROM THE INSIDE

A 1979 paper published by a team of scientists and doctors was titled "Psychosomal Dwarfism," derived from *psyche*, meaning *the mind*, and *soma*, meaning *body*. As their findings suggested, the growth of our body is influenced by the thoughts in our minds. Similarly, a 1984 paper titled "Psychosocial Dwarfism" said a child's delayed intellectual and social developments were spurred by the brain's interpretation of emotional deprivation.

These research studies showed, if nothing else, that our response to the things happening around us is a result of how our mind interprets the events that we are experiencing. Complete wellness comes first from the mind. Our body flourishes when our mind is filled with positivity. As an example, if in the face of challenges, you see opportunity, and in times of social distancing, you find ways to practice distant socializing, then you will respond in a more positive way to the events happening around you. Your smiles will be cheerful, and your thoughts will be positive.

A SUITABLE ENVIRONMENT MATTERS

In the quest to find total wellness, many people focus on personal mental development, physical fitness, and spirituality, neglecting their environment. The type of environment that you expose yourself to can significantly affect your chances for growth. As the researchers found, you may experience a decrease in growth when you are in an unfavorable environment. So, while you spend so much time and effort at the gym, meditating, and reading, your immediate environment may be creating a block for you.

The concept of the environment has changed over time. In the last generations, when people talked about the environment, they referred to your neighborhood, the people that you hung out with, and the schools you attended. In today's world, our environment is much more complicated. It does not only include the neighborhood that you find yourself in and the schools that your kids attend. You should also consider the digital spaces where you spend most of your time and the content that you consume. They make up our immediate environment today. In the next chapter, you will understand our modern-day environment better and how it impacts your chances of achieving all-around wellness.

FUNCTIONAL (OR PHYSICAL) FITNESS ISN'T WELLNESS

In 2019, United States' swimming hero Michael Phelps tweeted about his struggle with depression and anxiety. He advised that people should seek help when they need it and not wait on things. He has been a mental health advocate since then. Phelps is one of the most functionally fit athletes in the world despite his past records of DUI (driving under the influence).

In 2021, the reality that physical or functional fitness is not a sign of complete wellness became glaring when tennis player Naomi Osaka withdrew from the French Open for mental health reasons. According to the *LA Times*, she had "suffered long bouts of depression" since 2018.[4]

During the 2021 Summer Olympics in Tokyo, American gymnast Simone Biles refused to participate in several games because she had twisties, a sudden loss of body control while in the air. According to professionals, this is caused by "a lack of communication between the brain and body."[5] I extend my heartfelt support toward Phelps, Osaka, Biles, and every athlete battling with some form of mental health challenge. While they may be financially stable, functionally and physically fit, and socially strong, many of them, just like the rest of us, have some wellness hurdles to overcome.

The coronavirus pandemic made these hurdles higher to jump. Locked down for eighteen-plus months with terrifying information circulating in the news, we've been forced to deal with our thoughts alone. Many of us may have families to be with, while some are all alone. Organizations with nonessential workers promoted remote working while over forty-nine million Americans lost their jobs in the first three months of the lockdown.[6] This reality sent a lot of people into a downward spiral of unwellness, depression, and worries about an uncertain future.

With concern about their physical and mental health, a significant proportion of people (31 percent) engaged in more physical fitness activities, meditation, and yoga.[7] These activities helped many people overcome psychological issues that were being aggravated by overdependence on social media for recreation. As organizations began to open their doors slowly and some people took very cautious steps back into their usual lives, more people embraced physical fitness than they did prior to the pandemic.

As you may have noticed from the graphical illustration of the global wellness market above, the physical activity sector is the second largest in 2020. That shows how much many of us were investing in our physical health and are still doing so. Some aim to simply stay fit or build their dream bodies. Others are approaching physical activities as a wellness approach, or a part of it. Whatever the case, physical fitness is only a slice of the big wellness pie.

I won't encourage you to neglect your physical health. It is important for you to stay functionally fit. There is a sense of self-fulfillment that comes from being able to work on your body in ways that help you feel and look good. Also, having optimally functional body organs is everyone's hope and need. You need that too. Being physically fit might elevate your self-esteem, while a thick body could make another person feel more comfortable. Whichever body type you seek to maintain, I'm pretty sure that you look beautiful just the way you are. You shouldn't mistake a skinny or thick body for wellness or otherwise.

Regardless of your reasons for working out, being slim or thick is not a clear sign of sound mental or physical health. There's more to it than meets the eye. In the following pages, we will address the important things to look out for when finding balance in life and becoming well-rounded people with sound minds, financial independence, good physical health, thriving careers, and closely linked social networks.

> Regular check-ups with the doctor may confirm that you are healthy if you are eating a balanced diet, exercising regularly, getting enough sleep, and remaining free from illness. But this does not equal complete wellness.

WELLNESS IS PURPOSE DRIVEN

Some of us are working at our dream jobs, in nice organizations, and with amazing teams. We have lovely kids, amazing friends, and a comfortable financial status. Yet many are caught in a net of frustration and confusion. Some are sinking in their own emotions of fear, worry, or deep-seated rage. This is familiar to many and is troubling, to say the least.

In a typical workplace, every day at work is characterized by an endless flow of challenges, meetings, and the need for problem-solving abilities. To take it a step further, there's always a boss that you don't seem to be in sync with. Or a colleague with whom you often get off on the wrong foot. As long as we are individuals with varying beliefs, backgrounds, and personal values, it is normal for us to fall out of line with each other. What aggravates this divergence in shared spaces is the lack of clear communication. Some people have several meetings lined up each day with a stream of personal issues demanding their attention almost at the same time. Some are parents attending to children amid long Zoom meetings. Others may have an ill pet or aging parents to care for.

Not realizing and acknowledging these differences between us can lead to frustration, which often leads to irritation and rage (when dealing with colleagues) or ill-founded fear (when it involves a boss). These emotions are what Daniel Goleman referred to as *Destructive Emotions,* the title of his 2008 book.

Before the coronavirus pandemic, we thrived in the traditional workplace where we had to collaborate more in person. Now that the remote work environment is a new normal, you might assume that there is less frustration to deal with. That's not very true. Despite the dread of managing fellow humans, there is beauty in socializing with others. Our level of frustration has increased significantly in the remote work environment. According to a *Harvard Business Review* article, this may happen because many people are hyper-alert and are not exercising enough natural easiness when dealing with work-related issues.[8] Some are not allowed to work in a style that is best suited for them. The decline in the use of nonverbal communication has also added to the stress that staffers deal with. Now, many people are stuck in Zoom meetings, wading through endless to-do lists amid personal responsibilities. For these myriad reasons, a lot of staffers are unhappy and disengaged from their work.

Even though these are normal situations, these situations are aggravated when we lack clarity of purpose. We are more likely to find self-fulfillment when our jobs are aligned with our purpose at any given time. With a clear purpose, we make more satisfying decisions, are more productive, and live happier lives. In other words, we have a better chance at wellness when we identify a clear purpose for ourselves.

The first step to finding a fulfilling purpose for yourself is knowing what a purpose really means. Many people mistake purpose for measurable goals, ambitions, and desires. But, one's true purpose is more than that. It is a culmination of two simple aspects of our lives. According to Richard Davidson, a professor of psychology and psychiatry at the University of Wisconsin, purpose is the degree to which we understand our aims and personal values, and how well we are able to incorporate them into our everyday lives.[9] The reason why personal values should be considered in defining your purpose is that it helps answer the question of "why you are doing what you are doing?" Those who lose their "why" are still capable of living and thriving in the life that they choose. But, according to Dr. Joseph Castleberry, president of Washington's Northwestern University, these people are likely to drift from their primary purpose and get distracted by the small, easy wins of life.[10] Ergo, they often experience that familiar feeling of loss and emptiness and have difficulty retracing their steps.

> Without a purpose, our passion is often misplaced, as well as our values. We may take actions that make us feel good at the time, but that could push us away from who we truly are. Discover your purpose. Set your values and goals. Prioritize. And take actions that are aligned with your purpose.

Every day, we are responsible for making decisions that could shift our balance on the wellness scale. If we do not have a clear purpose that aligns with our personal values to guide our decisions, we could swerve and swirl around our wellness paths. The good news is that we can put a stop to that. You can do better. You can find your purpose and reach a sound state of well-being. Tony Robbins has spent a significant part of his life teaching people how to find their purpose and achieve happiness in life. According to Robbins, finding happiness in life starts with gratitude. You can either be thankful for what you have or worry about the things you don't. But those who always look at life with gratitude always seem to find purpose and happiness.

Effective time management isn't left out either. Life can be overwhelming when we have so much to take care of in a single day. Prioritizing and setting SMART goals that help us manage our time effectively will make all the difference between success of purpose and several episodes of distress. In the pages that follow, you will get to know more about setting SMART goals, managing time, and developing the right skills to help you build a healthier life.

CREATIVITY CAN IMPROVE YOUR WELL-BEING

There is no greater pressure than the one experienced by soldiers at war. Even more intense was the task of being Britain's First Lord of the Admiralty during World War II. Winston Churchill was tasked with bringing Britain back from the brink of defeat against the Germans. As history has it, he brought the Brits to victory. Behind the scenes, however, Churchill's brilliant war decisions were facilitated by his creative endeavors. He created time to paint and write despite the enormous pressure that he faced.[11]

In today's highly competitive world, the pressure to accomplish our goals both at work and in our immediate environment is crushing. For this reason, many of us experience chronic stress that affects our mental health and our ability to think critically and socialize with others. Constant stress pushes us into defensive mode and constant self-doubt. These emotions have ripple effects because we are very likely to hurt people's feelings when we act defensively toward them. Also, most people are less likely to accept informational feedback for this reason. However, creating time to perform creative activities can bring you closer to better well-being.

A study during the pandemic by Margaret Hiburn-Arnold, PhD, of the University of Texas at San Antonio, found that practicing creative arts can help us gain a sense of competence, autonomy of thought (self-dependent thinking), and an open attitude. When practiced with others, it enhances collaboration and development of supportive and meaningful relationships with other stakeholders.[12] So, regardless of the pressure that you may be facing today, you still have the chance to improve your wellness by dedicating some time to creative activities, like dancing, journaling, sketching, painting, cooking, pottery, etc.

Another study published in the *Journal of Positive Psychology* shows that engaging in creative activities daily is a path to living a flourishing life.[13] You do not need to be an expert at these activities, though. The flexibility and freedom of thought that they bring can help you relax and keep destructive emotions at bay. According to psychologist Cathy Malchiodi, PhD, creative activities can increase positive emotions and reduce symptoms of depression, stress, and anxiety, which are some of the emotions that keep us heavy-laden.

CURIOSITY AND WELLNESS

Kids are some of the loveliest people to be around. Have you noticed that too? Have you ever wondered why?

There's something about kids that brightens up my day and fills me with sentiments of love, care, and compassion. Their cheerful and easy-peasy lifestyle is contagious to many people. But if you pay close attention, you may find out that curious kids are often the ones with this uplifting aura. The ceaseless inquisitiveness of the "whys," "whats," and "hows" contributes significantly to this indescribable feeling of happiness.

Since the beginning of civilization, human survival has been dependent on our ability to learn new things and adapt to changing environments. Most of the life-changing discoveries and technologies that we use today are products of curiosity, and the discoverers, in most cases, lived pretty inspiring lives. The same was made evident during the coronavirus pandemic. Those that were curious and actively sought information reported greater well-being.[14]

The relationship between these two may appear new to you, but it's quite basic. We are all humans (except the Terminator), and we thrive by seeking novelty. In school or at work, the more cheerful people are the ones keen on learning how and why things happen. Consequently, they report greater performance, engage more with others and the projects at hand, and learn faster and better. The reason is simple. Curiosity. They want to find out more. They are seeking the "aha" moment that sends a rush of dopamine to the brain. And not only are curious people more informed, research shows that they show higher levels of positive emotion, lower signs of anxiety, and better general well-being.[15]

Our social well-being isn't left out. Many people who have a deep understanding of the people around them tend to build stronger relationships with them. In the workplace, for instance, you are more likely to build a deep connection with people from other cultures and socioeconomic backgrounds if you understand them well enough. This empathy for others was, at some point, developed out of curiosity. The wonder of what life is like on the other side of the wall. To be an emotionally intelligent and empathetic person, you need to be curious, actively listen to other people's stories, understand their perspectives, and associate with them accordingly.

People are naturally drawn to those that understand and care about their perspectives because they are less self-centered, less defensive, and less likely to demean the people around them.[16] Also, curious people tend to be wittier, more playful, and bond emotionally with strangers more easily. If you get them to open up, they are less boring, too, because their curiosity has likely exposed them to lots of exciting information to talk about. Nevertheless, you don't have to be an information junkie, gunning for sensitive details. Just knowing or expressing a genuine desire to know and care about the people you meet is enough to make them feel comfortable around you.

Curiosity alone may not be as powerful as researchers often make it out to be. Simply wanting to know something doesn't automatically increase your chance at wellness. But combined with determination, curiosity is a very potent tool for living a happier life. Do you recognize that dogged determination that curious kids show when they really need an answer to one of their sixteen million questions (sarcasm intended)? That's the kind of determination you should look forward to developing.

> Always ask questions and actively search for answers. You don't have to worry about asking the wrong questions because there are none. The search for answers gives you a sense of purpose. Finding answers brings fulfillment.

Interestingly enough, being a curious person facilitates the effect of other activities that are regularly construed as wellness-oriented. Even with healthy nutritional habits and constant exercise, your level of curiosity greatly influences your chances of wellness. In 2020, during the lockdown, high sugar intake increased anxiety and symptoms of depression in people with relatively low curiosity traits. In chapter three, you will learn how to enhance your curiosity traits and position yourself for better well-being.

INSIGHT IS GOLDEN

Curiosity inspires you to learn about others, your environment, and the world we all call home. It has even inspired others to explore beyond the clouds that we see and dream beyond our universe, the Milky Way. But all these curiosities have little to do with the knowledge of self. Socrates, the ancient Greek philosopher, once gave the timeless advice, "Man, know thyself."

Knowing yourself is referred to as insight, a word adapted from Medieval English. It simply means *inner sight*. According to Richard Davidson, it means having a healthy sense of yourself. With good insight, you will know what makes you tick and what rocks your boat. You will also have the awareness of how you have responded to events that unexpectedly slowed down your progress, swerved your positivity in the other direction, or pushed you out of balance temporarily. Why is this knowledge of self important?

With a healthy knowledge of yourself, you can deflect self-defeating narratives and find ways to get yourself back on track with whatever goal you are pursuing. According to a study, people with a stronger knowledge of self have higher tendencies to recover quickly from ugly experiences. They do this by reviewing within themselves how those negative experiences have affected their balance and activate their predefined coping mechanisms to bounce right back to normal, all within a short period.

> **Coping mechanisms** are the thoughts or behaviors that we use to reduce stress or the effect of shocks. We all have individual and social coping mechanisms. Some of us are more conscious of them than others. But the more conscious you are of yours, the better you will be at managing them.

Other than recovering from unpleasant experiences, insight is valuable in several other areas of our personal lives. A lot of people are troubled with self-doubt. Having clear insight can help you identify your strengths and challenges. Then you can harness your strengths for the greater good and acknowledge your challenges. Knowing these, you can seek help when you need it and offer to assist others in ways that are within your strengths.

With clear insights, you can calibrate your confidence and manage your expectations and the expectations of those around you more accurately. Knowing where and how you perform best, you will be more likely to make projections and cultivate the expectations of your boss, your colleagues, and your spouse in such a way that they will always rely on you because you're able to meet their expected outcomes/desires and stay true to your words more often than not. This well-calibrated confidence that others have in you can greatly improve your self-confidence, engagement at work, and performance. Therefore, with better insight, you will feel much better and, ultimately, let fewer people down over time.

PROGRESS VERTICALLY AND SPREAD LOVE IN ALL DIRECTIONS

Studies have shown that the mind is the most powerful tool of all. Yet people endlessly invest in physical activities, beauty products, and other products or services that are grouped under the wellness umbrella. The market for such products and services has grown faster than the biggest economies of the world in the last five years, but we still crave better well-being. Don't get me wrong; looking good and fit is a good business that everyone should take seriously. However, we should be more focused more on our internal environment, our minds, and how they are affecting our well-being.

Our external environment matters. Believe it or not, our external environment matters more than we've ever imagined. Investing in your physical and mental well-being may show good results wherever you find yourself. But in the right environment, the outcome of your efforts can be miraculous. Take the time to find other spaces and explore your chances at a better life.

There are some things that you just can't run from. We are all called to serve a purpose on Earth. Your purpose could be as big as making man an interplanetary species, eradicating malaria in Africa, or even as modest as helping the homeless in your community start to build better lives for themselves. As long as it is aligned with your personal values, you have a good shot at attaining wellness, albeit with a clearer understanding of the several areas of wellness, which is the purpose of this book.

In the midst of your busy schedule, do not neglect your need to stay creative. Have fun in ways that seem best. Allow your mind to try things on its own. Loosen up to dance, paint a picture, journal your thoughts, write a novel, or try your hand at sculptural arts, even architecture. You don't have to be a professional in any of these fields. You just need to let your mind do creative things. It helps ease the stress that most of us are constantly experiencing in this rapidly changing world.

As you create magic, don't forget to explore new things. Learn ceaselessly. Wonder. Ask questions. And cultivate the determination to seek answers to the questions that are pricking your mind. You can begin with random google searches and experience the small excitements that come from satisfying your curiosity. And, most importantly, in all your knowing, know thyself. There are things about you that can't be answered by Google but only by yourself. Take the time to self-reflect and develop a close relationship with yourself. This can be transformational in almost every part of your life. Give it a try and nudge yourself further to know more. And more you shall most definitely know.

In the next chapter, you will understand the pillars of wellness and acquire the knowledge that will help you put various aspects of your life under your personal magnifying lens. You will become familiar with the different levels of wellness and identify those that you need to work on improving.

Key Takeaways

1. Wellness starts from the mind and is heavily influenced by our environment.

2. Being physically fit is not the same as being well. Wellness requires more than regular engagement in physical activities, although it is a part of it.

3. You are more likely to attain lasting wellness and maintain balance when you discover your life's purpose.

4. Creatively pursuing your purpose and actively seeking knowledge (answers to questions) can make you a happier and more satisfied person.

5. Improving self-awareness through self-reflection will help you to know yourself better.

CHAPTER TWO

The 8 Pillars of Wellness

What do you consider the most important wellness activity? Is it your time at the gym or the distance run uphill? Is it the hours spent meditating or the low-carb diet that you've been sticking to for years? Whatever it may be, many people are very likely to misunderstand the scope of their well-being.

Our wellness requires a holistic approach because tilting toward one wellness activity at the expense of others does us more harm than good. For instance, within the space of physical well-being, there is a popular misconception that exercising frequently can make up for unhealthy eating habits. So, a lot of people focus on either eating well or exercising often. On a broader wellness scale, some people spend much of their time meditating and fortifying themselves spiritually while neglecting their need for financial stability.

To provide balanced well-being, we all need to pay adequate attention to the eight areas of our lives that affect our wellness. These areas are what I refer to as the Pillars of Wellness. This chapter is focused on describing these pillars individually to help you understand how each of them plays a part in your wholeness and ability to thrive in our rapidly changing world. At the end of this chapter, you will be able to identify the areas of your life that require a little more attention than you've been giving them. You will also be more attuned to the unique characteristics of people who are doing well in these areas of their lives.

EMOTIONAL WELLNESS

Many centuries ago, renowned philosophers like Plato and Descartes admonished our susceptibility to emotions. Even Plato referred to emotions as "foolish counselors." Although they influence our decisions and behaviors illogically, they are a part of us, and we can't do without them. Their importance in our lives cannot be overemphasized.

As humans, we are emotional beings. That means that our decisions, judgments, actions, and memories are influenced by emotions. Your ability to retain information, for instance, is higher when your emotional attachment to the subject is significant. Things that we are not emotionally drawn to rarely matter to us. Our emotions are also powerful enough to dictate the fruitfulness of our days. Many of us have a habit of checking our emails first thing in the morning. An unpleasant email has the potential to swing our mood in a negative way, and without strong control, our entire day could be ruined. Contrarily, exciting news, like a new job offer or acceptance to Harvard or your favorite HBCU, can make you feel elated all through the week. However, emotions transcend our individual selves. They are highly contagious.

Do you recall any time your boss or close colleague arrived physically at work or started a virtual work meeting in a not-so-lively mood? Did you ever notice how the mood quickly swept across the shared space, sending even the most excited staff into an inexplicable state of somberness? Well, that's an example of everyone getting infected by negative emotions. And when people emanate such emotions too often, they can be avoided. In pop culture, they are often called "bad vibes."

Because emotions are expressly felt in the mind with their effects traveling through the body cells, they are believed to define our psychology or mental well-being. A constant feeling of inadequacy, for example, can lead to anxiety and depression that significantly affects our psychological state. Frequent bursts of excitement and anticipation, on the other hand, can make someone come off as a person that people like to have around. Fortunately, though, we can define our emotions just as much as they define us. You can find a balance for things. You can keep the negative emotions at bay and effectively regulate your mood swings. Your ability to recognize, understand, and control your emotions is what is referred to as **emotional wellness**.

A widely known definition of emotional wellness is your ability to express your feelings in a healthy way, adjust your mind to the challenges that life throws at you, and cope with the almost regular stress that comes from living from day to day. To be able to accomplish all these things, you need to gain control over your thoughts and understand your innate personality.

If you take a look around, you will find that the leaders that you wish to emulate are emotionally intelligent. They always find a way to stay afloat amid life's challenges and everyday stressors. And they transmit an aura of assurance to everybody around them. It's the reason that you and a dozen other staff want to be like them. How do they manage to do that?

It takes seven important skill sets to maintain a high level of emotional wellness.

Self-awareness: As discussed in the last chapter, knowing yourself makes all the difference. It is the foundation for a life that's full of self-fulfillment. Take measures to improve your self-awareness, recognize the various emotions that you feel, and identify what makes you feel in those ways. Whenever you feel distressed, you should understand that it's not the first time that you're feeling that way, and it probably won't be the last time. Being aware of what made you feel that way can help you prevent or redirect it in the future.

Self-acceptance: After coming to the full awareness of what you are feeling, it's important to accept it. Acknowledge the fact that you are human and emotions are ingrained into your being. Then you can be at peace with yourself, not allowing environmental factors to create turmoil within you.

Expression and self-care: Accepting that you're hurt or excited is a good thing to do. However, holding it within yourself is not advisable. Suppressing your emotions can have damaging effects on your physical and mental health.[1]

So, do yourself a favor and let it out. Express that joy. Let your colleagues know that you are unhappy about their behavior toward you. However, make sure to express these emotions in healthy ways that are respectable to the people around you. According to Amy Gallo's article in the *Harvard Business Review*, it's important for you to recognize and acknowledge how you might have stirred up unpleasant behavior from your colleagues.[2] Then you have to manage your reactions, because simply lashing out won't help the situation in any way. And don't forget to share your thoughts with them in the best way you can, after detaching yourself from the behavior so that your emotions don't get the better of you.

Emotional agility: People with a high emotional quotient have the ability to summon positive emotions and avoid things that could trigger negative emotions. This is a superpower that you should try to develop. Your ability to swing away from unwanted feelings can help you thrive through times of rapid changes. Reading an unpleasant email first thing in the morning may ruin your day, but being able to put it behind you quickly and get into the wave of things will help you stay productive throughout the day.

Integrity: People with sound emotional well-being are up-front about their abilities. They let you know what they can't do early enough to avoid getting invested in an emotionally draining engagement. They don't try to please everyone and have well calibrated expectations of others. With these, they can prevent the unpleasant heartbreaks that come with unmet expectations.

Coping skills: Respected leaders who make their well-being a priority develop coping skills to help them get through even the worst days. Some use this opportunity to integrate physical activities into their mental and emotional wellness routines by taking a run or a long walk to relieve themselves.

Stress management: Stress is a precursor of mental distress, anxiety, and even depression. Considering the competitive landscape of businesses, as well as the increasing demands on parents and caregivers, staffers are constantly exposed to stress, and the few people that have excellent stress management skills are more likely to maintain optimum mental well-being despite the strains that they face from everyday work life.

Your ability to combine these seven skills and create a commitment to improving them daily will bring you closer to sounder mental and emotional well-being both in your professional and personal life.

To improve your emotional (or psychological) wellness, you should:

- Recognize your feelings (i.e., identify anger, distinguish infatuations from actual passion, get familiar with excitement and anxiety, etc.).

- Accept that you are human. Those emotions are part of being human. Don't deny them.

> - Express what you are feeling in healthy ways. Find a controlled space to scream if that makes you feel better. Respectfully talk to someone about how they make you feel. Etc.
> - Let go of negative emotions and embrace positive emotions by focusing your mind on the present and on things that make you feel good.

SOCIAL WELLNESS

The proverbial "show me your friends" statement hasn't been affected by changing times. Associating with happier people has its way of making you happy. Similarly, young adults are more likely to try hard drugs the first time if they build relationships with other adults that abuse drugs.

In a study of first-year medical students, researchers from Massey University in New Zealand found that a healthy friendship significantly increased the rate of assimilation.[3] This means that by studying as a group, students excel more. In the workplace, a group project is more likely to succeed than a solo project. In entrepreneurship, organizations launched with two or more cofounders are 30 percent more likely to succeed than those with a single founder.[4]

Like emotions, relationships define us. And being able to build healthy relationships matter a lot to your professional and personal well-being. A strong social network can positively affect your life span, help you manage stress more effectively, develop a stronger immune system, and reduce the risks of cardiovascular diseases.[5] So, while your mental health is essential, your social life should be at the center of your wellness activities.

Wellness in a social sense is your ability to interact with those around you through effective communication, development of meaningful relationships, and respect for self and others. This ability is principal to creating solid support systems that can help you thrive through life's challenges, especially in rapidly changing times like the post-pandemic era. To nurture this ability, you should consider the following:

Define your values. This important aspect of our social lives is often neglected. Many people, especially young ones, rush into building relationships without clearly defining their values. The consequences of ignoring this vary. For one, we are leaving our lives to the tides of chance. Some lucky people may build strong bonds with honorable people that have their values in place. Some others may get entangled in unhealthy relationships that could shape how they perceive society. You can avoid this easily by defining your values early on and sticking to them. Finding really good friends and comrades is significantly easier when your values are well defined.

Be more outgoing. In today's world, you meet a lot of people virtually. Some of these people go on to become really close friends with whom you play virtual games like online trivia, chess, or *Call of Duty*. You may even meet with them in person over the years. Heck, you might even be like me and decide to meet up virtually through apps like Peloton, Weight Watchers, virtual yoga, dance, Minecraft coding classes, or more. However, the digital space slows down your social development.

As vaccines have become available and people are starting to engage more in person once more, you can meet up in person for dinner, group workouts, and many other events. This will increase your chances of finding satisfaction in yourself. Those who are physically connected to their friends and family are happier than other people relying on electronic platforms.[6] So, as activities slowly return to normal, it's important that you take safety measures, including vaccinations, when going out to experience a touch of physical connection once again.

Practice self-disclosure. Don't be too uptight. Loosen up and allow people to know you. When you connect with other people, take the opportunity to tell them about yourself, your background, your ambitions, and other information that you believe is safe to share. People want to be friends with those that they know. And strangers become friends as they get to know themselves. Ensure that you do your part in building the friendship bond.

Actively listen to others. While you tell people about yourself, don't forget to pay undivided attention to the people you are connecting with. Building a social network goes both ways. Inasmuch as you want them to know how cool you are, give them the opportunity to disclose information about themselves. You might learn a few things about your new friends that can help you connect with them better. Alternatively, by actively listening, you might discover that their self-disclosure reveals a few red flags that are in conflict with your predefined values. Remember, everyone can't be your friend. When you find out, through active listening, that someone you met is not appropriate for your well-being, make sure to show them good respect and be outspoken and compassionate.

Keep in touch. Did you ever take the contact information of the eloquent guy that you met at the café two weeks ago? You should try to stay in touch with your old buddies and new acquaintances alike. Don't be withdrawn from people. Withdrawal could lead to isolation and depression. It doesn't matter if you've been losing touch for a while. Now is a good time to make amends. Pick up your phone and call or text them. Let them know that they are in your thoughts. It's easier to rekindle dormant relationships than to find and make new friends.[7]

Join groups, clubs, or organizations. Find clubs and organizations with values that are closely aligned with yours. If you are inclined to save the planet by planting trees, you can consider joining an environmental organization. If you are a lover of chess, soccer, basketball, books, or others, you should try finding and joining an appropriate club. There are many virtual gatherings that are well suited to accommodate various people with similar interests. These include small virtual chess clubs, online communities, and several others. To get a little breath of physical connection, there are some places offering outdoor sports like tennis and basketball. However, they are strictly following COVID-19 safety protocols. So, ensure that you are vaccinated and follow the laid-out protocols while visiting and using these facilities.

> Social wellness is achievable when you:
>
> - Have values that you live by.
> - Explore opportunities to safely connect with people that you share common values with.
> - Listen to others and empathize with them.
> - Put in the effort to maintain healthy relationships by keeping in touch.

ENVIRONMENTAL WELLNESS

In 2019, while the Amazon rainforest was caught up in high-rising wildfires, a Brazilian couple, Sebastião and Lélia Salgado, was celebrated worldwide for planting 2.7 million trees in two decades.[8] It is the most that a single individual (or couple) has done for the environment. Why is it so important?

This planet is ours. It's the only home that we've known since the beginning of time. Our immediate environment affects our lives in every way. Recall the study by the German doctors in chapter two. The child's ability to produce growth hormones was greatly inhibited by the environment that he was living in. The cure to his dwarfism was a simple change of environment.

Intellectually, our lives are shaped by the environment. Children learn from their surroundings, and the knowledge that they acquire sticks with them for almost a lifetime.[9]

You are responsible for optimizing your environment to deliver adequate stimulation for improving the cognitive development of those you care about. For this reason, some parents move to a new environment that can better stimulate the development of their children.

Other than growth hormone production, the environment has a significant influence on your spiritual well-being. Depending on your beliefs, culture, and values, the components of the environment that have the highest relevance to your spirituality vary. For many, mineral rocks, like crystals, which are a product of our environment, are an embodiment of purity, faith, and perfection.[10]

Your environmental well-being is intertwined with physical wellness as well. Engaging in fitness activities in a healthy environment is great. However, a highly polluted and hot environment with uneven topography can make outdoor fitness activities unbearable. You may not be able to change the topography of your street, but you can contribute significantly to the reduction of pollution and heat by planting trees and engaging in other environmental wellness activities, which also have positive impacts on your mind, body, and soul.

By definition, you are environmentally well if you occupy a pleasant and stimulating environment that supports your well-being and growth as an individual.[11] However, with the exception of being pollution-free and optimally stimulating, an environment conducive to well-being is relative. You may find high-profile neighborhoods boring, while another person could consider The Bronx to be too stimulating. Whatever the case, you are responsible for helping create the environment that you want to live in, one which you find self-fulfilling and conducive to your well-being.

Due to socioeconomic constraints, some people may experience challenges in changing their environment. Many people living in public housing would really appreciate having a lush home to themselves in a safe and secure neighborhood. It turns out that there is little that can be done, considering the available resources. But you can do something to create an environmentally buoyant life for yourself and your loved ones.

For one, focusing on your home environment can be a good start. Create a safe routine that shields your children from traumatizing incidents that might be happening around the neighborhood. Healthy household rules are equally important. Some homes try to see that everyone speaks in a moderate tone by prohibiting children from yelling at each other.

Visual works of art are useful for helping everyone at home engage in creative activities. Taking some hours to color with the kids can give them an opportunity to build resilience toward challenges that the exterior environment is posing. And in the case of traumatizing events like gunfire in and around bad neighborhoods, incorporating meditation into your household's daily routine could be really helpful. So, no matter the situation of your external environment and socioeconomic status, you can create an environment suitable for growth and wellness.

To help you shoulder the responsibilities of improving your environment, take the following into account.

Environmental awareness. In a time like this, it is dangerous for us to be oblivious to our immediate environment. You should take the time to develop a strong awareness of the environment that you live in. Take the time to identify the elements of nature around you and make decisions that can enhance their sustainability. Remember that nature has therapeutic and soothing functions. You don't imagine yourself meditating in an environment emanating unpleasant smells, do you?

Environmental awareness doesn't end at your recognition of nature's wonderful elements. It transcends your ability to personalize it. You need to figure out how these natural elements around you affect your functionality as a human being. Do they help you to stay productive? Do they reduce the frequency with which you visit the doctor? Is your environment conducive enough for your children's cognitive development?

It's your responsibility to identify these effects, as well as the elements that are causing them. If an element is inhibiting your well-being or that of your loved ones, it's always advisable to remove the element or consider how you could use it to a positive end.

Environment redesigning. The setting of our immediate environment can significantly affect our ability to carry out everyday activities.[12] Studies have shown that our behaviors toward work, ourselves, and the people around us are influenced by the environment that we find ourselves in. Many people living in public housing, for instance, might keep their guard up and reduce their propensity for spending lavishly while a flush neighborhood may inspire the direct opposite.

On a more personal level, our environment dictates the habits that we cultivate. In his book *Atomic Habits*, James Clear shares studies showing that having a soda-filled refrigerator makes it easier to consume more sodas than you may have intended to. Consequently, for someone trying to quit smoking, the chances of success are slimmer if you have cues loitering around your environment. Similarly, having a bottle of water on your desk at all times will help increase your daily intake of water. You might be wondering where this is going, and that's okay. Keep reading.

Knowing your wellness goals, you can redesign your environment to help you live the self-fulfilling life that you've always wanted. Keep a book within sight to always remind you to build your intellectual well-being. Make unhealthy elements hard to access to reduce your propensity to use or have them.

Selfless thinking. No matter how small an environment is, it will be occupied by others. If you are a parent, your home environment needs to be favorable for growth. If you're not a parent and are probably living alone, you may assume that it's all about you. Well, it's not. When people visit you, sometimes unexpectedly, they want to be in a healthy environment. Nonsmokers may find it grossly discomforting to sit in a room covered in tobacco smell. When redesigning your environment, take others into consideration. Think about how they can thrive in the space that you are creating. Solving this puzzle can greatly improve your social network as well as emotional well-being.

Selflessness doesn't have to be toward humans alone. The plants and animals around us deserve our consideration as well. Think about the animals in the woods and the fish in the ocean. When engaging in activities, ensure that they do not affect these creatures' well-being negatively. Many organizations are revisiting their environmental practices because the world now understands how much we are affected by our suffering environment, and many are profiting immensely by doing the most for the environment.[13]

A forward-thinking mindset that allows you to consider how your actions may impact the future. Living in the moment is a pretty good thing when you are trying to make the most of your social life. However, it's not advisable when it comes to making environmental wellness decisions. Before taking actions that could directly impact the environment, step back to think about how your actions can affect the environment in the future, even though the immediate benefits are enticing. Some of the world's greatest environmental problems were born due to our failure to employ forward-thinking mindsets when making environmental decisions for personal and economic gains. But we know better now. And we can do better.

Reduce. Reuse. Recycle. In one way or another, we are contributing to the death of this beautiful planet. Now that we are aware of our shortcomings, we can give Earth a survival chance by reducing our use of products made from nonbiodegradable materials that are environmentally unfriendly. Make it a value to use more organic products and support businesses that are putting the safety of our environment first.

No matter how we think of them, plastics and metals are a part of our lives now. So, in our bid for wide adoption of eco-friendly products, we still need to fall back to plastics. It is advisable to only purchase plastics that you can reuse rather than those designed for one-time use only. According to the World Economic Forum, if we only reuse 10 percent of all the plastic that we buy today, almost half of the plastics polluting the ocean will be no more.[14] Imagine what we could achieve by just reusing half of all the plastics we throw away. Incredible!

However, should the need to dispose of eco-unfriendly products arise, it would be great to find ways to recycle them. The materials can be used to make other useful things. You can trade in your old stuff for newer things. This way, manufacturers can help recycle. You can also save some money from your purchases by simply trading in older, recyclable products.

Your journey to environmental wellness is easy when you:

- Recognize your feelings (i.e., identify anger, distinguish infatuations from actual passion, get familiar with excitement and anxiety, etc.)
- Accept that you are human. Those emotions are part of being human. Don't deny them.

- Express what you are feeling in healthy ways. Find a controlled space to scream if that makes you feel better. Respectfully talk to someone about how they make you feel. Etc.
- Let go of the negative emotions and embrace positive ones by focusing your mind on the present and things that make you feel good.

SPIRITUAL WELLNESS

Intentionally taking the life of another person is ethically and morally wrong. So is racism and all other types of discrimination. But how do people know that these activities are wrong? How does a five-year-old know that telling a lie is not a good thing to do?

We all have inborn moral checks and balances that help us tell right from wrong, good from evil. These balances inspire us to ask questions and to also accept that not all of our questions have answers, at least not at the moment. And most importantly, these checks and balances are shaped by our strongest and deepest beliefs.

At our core, we all have something great to believe in. Some of us were born into such beliefs, while others discovered and aligned theirs with a certain group. Regardless of the category that you may find yourself in, your core beliefs play a part in keeping you psychologically sound. We tend to recognize things, accept or deny practices, and build our life principles based on our beliefs, our innate understanding of good and evil. Taking steps or engaging in activities that are contrary to those deep-rooted beliefs could jolt our life's balance, sending us into a chaotic state of confusion and even depression.

To be spiritually well means to be connected (and stay connected) to something greater than yourself. It could be a supreme being (God), a supernatural deity of some sort, a deeply personal purpose, or a cause that is almost completely selfless (like philanthropy). This connection with whatever it is helps you create values, principles, morals, and beliefs that give you a sense of purpose. Remember that, according to Richard Davidson, to create a purpose that's truly fulfilling to pursue, your values and principles must align with your goals in ways that you deeply understand. With values and moral beliefs that are aligned with your personal and professional goals, decision-making becomes easier because, when given multiple choices, you will almost always choose options that are in line with your values and beliefs. And you will take actions that will reinforce these beliefs and values as well.

We are drawn to religion in its entirety. It's important for you to know, however, that religion is quite different from spirituality. First, you are an individual with personal convictions. We all are. And these convictions, which are entirely personal and may not be shared with others, define our spirituality. Religion, on the other hand, is a set of beliefs, morals, and principles shared by a community of people with whom their spiritualities align closely. Therefore, your spirituality, that personal conviction, informs your choice of religious affiliation. It inspires you to choose to become a Christian, Muslim, Jew, Hindu, or any religion that you feel more inclined to. It could inspire you to become an atheist as well.

There has been much raving about spirituality for as long as I can remember. My parents were strong advocates of spiritual beliefs, and they practiced them. According to the Pew Research Center, 84.4 percent of the world population is affiliated with a religious belief.[15] Why are so many people attached to their abstract spiritual beliefs? What benefits are they getting from this lifelong affiliation with communities of people that share similar beliefs and engage in similar activities to reinforce such beliefs?

The benefits are mostly personal and closely linked with improving psychological (or emotional) well-being. For one, religiosity and spirituality have been shown to reduce anxiety and prevent the drift into depression that often arises from several episodes of anxiety.[16] In clinical studies, religious activities and strong spirituality are two-edged swords. They help to facilitate recovery from depression and build resilience against the recurrence of depressive conditions. However, on the flip side, they could inspire ugly episodes of depression for insanely curious and detail-seeking practitioners.[17]

Nevertheless, you have a greater chance at happiness when you are deeply connected to your inner self through upstanding morals, principles, and values. A constant reinforcement of these values and moral beliefs makes you feel better about yourself. In fact, people who have a connection with something greater than them are happier than those who are chiefly focusing on themselves.[18] Also, they build stronger social connections with family and people that they meet.

Spirituality has shown important mental impacts on the cognitive well-being of those middle-aged and older. A majority of us are more likely to retain important youthful memories if we are spiritually sound. A study published in *The Gerontologist* revealed that spiritual involvement is capable of preventing cognitive decline in adults, which is one of the risks of aging.

On a societal level, a wide adoption of spiritual wellness activities can help maintain social order. Having values and morals set in place, we are more likely to hold ourselves accountable for actions that are not aligned with our purpose, even without expressing them openly. For that reason, people with sound spiritual well-being are less inclined to commit crimes that could harm others.[19]

Knowing all the interesting benefits of being spiritually well is not enough to anchor yourself to a greater purpose. Instead, taking action and making the commitment to strengthen your beliefs will make the difference that matters. Some activities to consider on this quest to spiritual prosperity aren't hidden from sight.

Explore your spiritual core by investing some time in meditation and personal reflection. Meditation allows you to experience your existence at a level that is beyond what you personally know.[20] Its connection with spirituality has been ages long. Buddha, for one, encourages followers to meditate because it's one way to keep yourself grounded in the present without worries about the past or anxiety about an unknown future. Personal reflection, which often happens during meditation, brings clarity of thought, which, according to Trinlay Rinpoche, is the real source of happiness and self-enhancement.[21]

Spend more time appreciating nature, absorbing its soothing spiritual essence. Nature is a sign that there are things greater than us, bigger than the things we know. By merely spending time with nature, you are likely to appreciate the existence of a supreme being who, as many believe, has a great concern toward you and the world that He has made. Besides the spiritual aspect, nature is a valuable source of inspiration. Creatives (like writers, artists, and designers) find it useful for overcoming creative blocks, which are a temporary inability to create optimally. It is a source of inspiration to many and an escape from most of life's challenges when you allow yourself to really savor it.

Practice mindfulness more often. As competition in the world increases, events are occurring at an incredibly fast pace. Many people are caught up in the swing of things and unable to get a hold of themselves. They are either worrying about a presentation that's due in a week or mulling over their performance at a seminar three days ago. All of these events can draw us away from our core principles, values, and morals, our cherished connection with our beliefs. By practicing mindfulness, you can be in the present more often than the world is allowing you to be. You can be less reactive or overwhelmed by the things happening around you. You can finally get a hold of yourself and be aware of what you are involved in. This can give you a sense of control over your life.

Volunteer for a cause that is greater than you alone, to support the sustainability of humankind. In a world where our happiness depends on our impact on the lives of others, providing valuable support to those that need it goes a long way toward creating spiritual satisfaction for those helping. Also, volunteering offers opportunities to create social relationships with people who share similar values with you, thereby playing a role in your social well-being. Selflessness does have its rewards, and you should give it a try.

Express gratitude for everything and nothing. Being thankful for the good things that you experience is considered a spiritual practice that helps you relish in the good times and stay positive. With more positive memories expressed through gratitude, you will be happier and more likely to attract more positive experiences to be grateful for and happy about. It's an endless cycle of positivity when you are grateful for both tangible and intangible goodness. From a social perspective, we are drawn to grateful people. We want to be with them because they appreciate us and the little things that we do. They make us feel like we truly matter. For that reason, a grateful person is more likely to build strong relationships and maximize his or her social well-being.

You may be tempted to link the impacts of spirituality to your mental and social well-being because I mentioned so much about their relationship. However, your spirituality determines how you respond to your environment, vocation, and even finances. Some people believe that giving is sowing seeds. Some others believe that giving your excesses to those in need helps you feel greater self-worth and happiness. This is the major driver for several philanthropic activities that the world has seen. Whatever the case, you should know that your spiritual well-being is just as important as maintaining functional kidneys. You don't have to take it for granted.

> Your spiritual journey may not necessarily be religious. Simply having a strong belief in something selfless, greater than yourself, requires collective effort (a movement) aligned with your purpose.
>
> There are several spiritual causes to pursue. Choosing one is personal. But whichever you choose, you won't be alone. There are people already pursuing that cause or who are willing to join you.

INTELLECTUAL WELLNESS

Has there been a time when you were entangled with a group of scholars, comrades, colleagues, or friends, discussing a subject that was completely alien to you? On the flip side, have you tried holding a conversation with someone and it turned out that they knew absolutely nothing about the subject that you were trying to discuss? Either way, the conversation usually winds up awkward and is often unpleasant to remember.

In the last chapter, I mentioned that curiosity is a tool for living a happier life. This is not true simply because it feels good to learn new things. Curiosity pushes you to learn more, to become intellectually sound. Enhanced intellectual well-being is a potent recipe for building a solid social network. Everyone needs to have a healthy relationship with a mentor, trusted advisor, and/or an enlightened friend to stay informed and inspired to learn more. Ironically, it's very unlikely you will make the acquaintance of an enlightened friend, mentor, and/or advisor if you have nothing intellectual to offer.

I've met people who have a habit of giving a scripted answer to questions that should inspire intellectual creativity. One of the frequent answers is *"I don't know."* I call this the I-don't-know syndrome, and it is very different from the Dunning-Kruger effect, which is the tendency for less competent people to overestimate their abilities while highly competent people do the exact opposite. Those with I-don't-know syndrome actually don't know, and they express no desire to know. They exude an aura of disinterest whenever a subject is outside their comfort zone. And it's saddening to know that they often pay the price for not knowing and being unconcerned. They are less likely to attract intellectually buoyant people and are often intimidated by their knowledgeable peers. That is a terrible state of intellectual well-being. First things first, though. What exactly does intellectual wellness really mean?

Intellectual wellness is your ability to engage in mentally stimulating activities, like healthy debates that could challenge your perspective, teaching and explaining what you've learned, and exploring the depths of knowledge at your disposal. It is also your ability to employ your knowledge for creative activities that can enhance your engagement with others and the community. It goes beyond your IQ and what you learn from school, although those are vital to your intellectual growth. To be intellectually well off, you need to be street smart, culturally informed, involved in community activities, and have elevated personal knowledge of things, people, and places. Of course, no one knows it all, but someone with considerable intellectual well-being knows something about a lot of things. And why is this versatile knowledge important?

Being knowledgeable makes you a better member of society. You know how and why certain things happen and therefore react in ways that are acceptable to society. In a diverse workplace, for instance, understanding the cultural background of your colleagues can help you associate better, respect boundaries, and build relationships that are mutually beneficial. Your ability to understand the laws governing your immediate environment is another way that intellectual wellness helps you live within society's acceptable norms and stay out of trouble.

Those who are intellectually unwell are more likely to adhere to a lifestyle that leans in one direction with little or no consideration for opposing perspectives. A lot of these lifestyle choices are seen in low socioeconomic neighborhoods, where hunger for knowledge is relatively low. However, being intellectually buoyant inspires the curiosity to explore new ideas that will enable you to develop your understanding of several aspects of life and allow you to live a balanced life. This is possible because your mind is open to exploring perspectives other than yours. Being intellectually healthy opens your mind to the possibility that you might be wrong. And if you happen to be right, it begs the question of how right you could be and inspires you to find the answers.

Measuring your degree of intellectual wellness is also a major challenge since there's no concrete way to quantify it. However, considering the Dunning-Kruger effect, people with low intellectual well-being are very likely to perceive themselves as very smart while the ones who are actually smart are swamped by the possibility that they could be wrong and, in fact, be dense in many ways. So, if you are thinking right now that you are a genius and the smartest person in your neighborhood, chances are that you are far from it. Whether you are genuinely smart, simply perceive yourself to be smart, or are struggling to place yourself in a specific position on the intellectual wellness scale, you can improve your cleverness in several areas. There are some ways that you could employ to make this happen.

Read. Read for fun. Read to satisfy your curiosity. For whatever reason, just read. Because the virtues of humanity's greatness are written in ink. Acquisition of knowledge is the first step to intellectual wellness and perpetual enlightenment. By reading, you expose your mind to the possibilities of the world around you. While you live a single lifetime, the lives of millions of other people, their experiences, studies, mistakes, and lessons, patterns of thinking, and intelligence are expressed through writings done either by themselves or those that knew them keenly. By reading books, you give yourself the opportunity to see the world through their lenses in ways that you might not get a chance to see otherwise.

Engage in healthy debates with friends, and open your mind to opposite perspectives. Many situations are not black and white. Between the polar edges, there are several shades of gray that we may not see when viewing those situations from the sides. By engaging in open conversations and healthy debates with those that have a different perspective, beliefs, thought patterns, and personal values, you can learn to see things in a different light, and you will then be able to validate the accuracy of your own knowledge. Sometimes we are wrong about our assumptions entirely or in part. Having these healthy debates helps you discover the leaks in your assumptions, offers an opportunity for you to research and learn more, and, in some cases, challenges you to reevaluate your assumptions and beliefs.

Journal regularly. When we think about solutions to the challenges around us, our minds isolate simple answers. Sometimes each of these simple answers won't solve the issues that boggle our minds. But combining two or more simple solutions that our minds have isolated can bring about the ultimate end of the issue. What's interesting, however, is that those very simple solutions that pop into our thoughts are very easy to forget or even dismiss. So, writing them down can help you keep track of them. With a thought journal, you can connect several simple solutions to come up with really viable solutions to complex problems.

Learn from mentors and coaches. This is a set of people who have won your respect and admiration and are worth emulating. You should get close to them and learn from them. Reading is great, but keep in mind that not every successful, intelligent person goes to the trouble of writing a book. So, if you have access to someone whose life you would love to model yours after, it's a smart choice to learn directly from them. Feel free to ask questions, share your perspectives with them, and welcome them to challenge your ideas. It will do you great good.

Solve puzzles and riddles. Puzzles and riddles challenge you to think outside the box and exercise your creative powers. The mind grows lazy when it lacks creative challenges. Routine activities are more likely to reduce your brain's agility, although they are less demanding. New, challenging mental tasks like puzzles and riddles stretch the mind to solve the problem before it. Being able to solve those riddles and puzzles has a healthy impact on the brain. Small wins like solving a simple riddle can trigger the release of a healthy dose of dopamine in the brain to help you feel happy with yourself.

Play games. It could be video games or board games. They have a helpful impact on your well-being.[22] Contrary to the belief that excessive gaming time can cause intellectual deterioration, people who spend more time gaming are seen to be more intellectually accurate. Among surgeons, those that played more video games made 37 percent fewer errors and completed procedures 27 percent faster than their non-video-game-playing peers.[23]

To be able to thrive intellectually, you need to acknowledge the fact that your knowledge is limited and be willing to let go of information that you previously believed in after you find it to be false or obsolete. Bear in mind that your social network plays a significant role in helping you gain access to certain types of information that could help you advance your personal, social, and career goals.

> Having access to information and communicating it effectively is very important to your relevance in life.
>
> Find learning opportunities and engage in activities that will increase your learning and comprehension speed.

OCCUPATIONAL WELLNESS

Whenever I enter a workplace anywhere, I often encounter a few staff members that appear to be down and unhappy, or at a minimum, with heavy things on their minds and in their hearts. I can always tell that they dread Mondays and look forward to Fridays. Even though they really want to contribute their best to the job that pays them a livable wage, they just can't seem to get themselves to perform optimally. The irony is that most of these people earn a handsome paycheck and work in an environment conducive to the kind of jobs that they do, and with a really lovely team. If you find yourself in such a situation at any time, you are likely to lose trust in your abilities, doubt your personal values, dislike your bosses, and even get irritated by unsuspecting colleagues.

Very often people resort to excuses and defensiveness. Sooner or later, as they run out of reasons for delivering a mediocre performance at the workplace, they loiter around in terror of losing their job or being embarrassed for their underperformance. This is not only affecting a small proportion of the workforce. It is a corporate epidemic. Fifty-one percent of Americans are unsatisfied and unhappy at their jobs, which is leading to gross underperformance, anxiety, and depression. On a global scale, the number is more troubling. Eighty-five percent of the world's full-time staff are disengaged from their work.[24, 25] But why aren't enough people speaking up?

It's difficult for staff to explain what they are really feeling because, for most, it sounds ungrateful to express your dissatisfaction with a job that is probably paying you above the industry average. It's not the organization's fault, and it's definitely not yours either. However, instead of finding faults, excuses, and ways to rekindle your excitement for the job, it's never a bad time to reconsider your occupational wellness in a career that you've chosen to pursue. Start with yourself. Take some moments of self-reflection and ask yourself a few questions in the line of:

Why did I take this current job?

Was it for a better paycheck or because it aligned with my personal values?

Why am I still here? For the same reason I took it in the first place, or has something changed?

What's making me unhappy? What should I do next?

These questions could open up your mind to consider the actual source of your disengagement from work. So far, there is only one reason why people find themselves in this position of unsettling occupational well-being. The jobs that they once loved, or chose to love, no longer (or never) align with their inborn personalities.

In a rapidly changing world like we have today, many people are forced into innovation, constantly changing work routines, new projects, changing colleagues, and more than a dozen digital tools to work with on every ongoing project. While this is exciting for staff members that are tech-savvy and love aesthetics, others get overwhelmed and are more at ease with a traditional and slow-changing environment. For most people, it is nearly impossible to walk up to a boss and ask to slow things down. Having this type of person work in a fast-growing tech start-up may bring endless episodes of anxiety and confusion. But a lot of people are jumping into tech without considering this part of their personality.

Another instance is seen in those who cherish security of job and pay. These people want to be certain that they will have a job in the next decade and that their retirement plan is in place. They don't want to wake up on Monday morning with the possibility of being out of a job on Friday hanging loosely at the back of their minds. On the flip side, there are people who love the allure of unpredictability. It keeps them on their toes and inspires them to take risks and explore opportunities for rapid growth. Keeping these people in routine work where the chances for rapid growth are slim and spontaneity is unlikely can send electric waves of frustration down their spine.

Therefore, in order to consider yourself occupationally well, it means that you have the ability to have a career that provides a feeling of purpose, productivity, and aligns with your personality traits. To be able to do this, you must first understand yourself and know how you respond to high risk, uncertainty, routine, discoveries, selflessness, and all others that could be a determinant for job satisfaction. Once you've checked the boxes, you might be wondering what comes next.

Find a mentor. With self-reflection and awareness, you probably already know your strengths and challenges. You also know your personal values and have set your career goals clearly. You know where you fit, what you love to do, and how you like to do it. Make a list of these unique qualities and search around to find someone that's doing the work you want to do better than the way you've ever thought of doing it. Make that person your mentor. They may be five thousand miles away, but who really cares about distance when the internet has brought us insanely close to each other?

A misconception, however, is that your mentor must know you in person. This is far from true. Sometimes we learn from people without ever making personal contact with them. If you look closely, those with successful careers often share their experience via blogs, LinkedIn, books, or other social media platforms. They share valuable knowledge and advice for those looking to follow their path. Take the time to follow them and stay on top of your pursuit for self-fulfillment.

> People with highly successful careers have mentors. Most are willing to mentor others as well. Find and connect with them.

FINANCIAL WELLNESS

Let's get imaginative for a moment. Arianna works three full-time jobs, each paying above minimum wage. She's a single mom to a smart teenage daughter, Edna. She (Arianna) is an advocate for equality, and she's respected for her strong beliefs in the cause as well as her admirable work ethic. It's a good Friday evening after a really busy week. Wine in hand, Ariana watches Edna open an envelope to find a letter from the University of California at Berkeley. She's been offered a provisional admission to study political science and American history. This is a big opportunity for both ladies, especially for Arianna, who has always hoped that her beloved Edna would earn a Juris Doctorate and go nose-deep into Washington-style politics. Now, Ariana can't afford the college fees, not with her current income.

And there are so few hours in a single day to work another full-time job to level up.

Although Arianna is excited about her daughter's good news, she reports to all three jobs absent-minded and disengaged for the next few weeks. As the deadline for acceptance of Edna's provisional admission draws near, the stress builds up. Why does Arianna work so hard yet can't afford her beloved daughter's college tuition? She either never really took the time to plan as a single parent or never had the opportunity to plan, given everything that she has had to grapple with. She's caught off-guard and backed into a financial corner that could cost her daughter's future.

This is an illustration with fictional characters, but the cap fits a lot of heads, many of whom are working long hours and living the lives you wish for. Despite the allure of luxury and the prestige of working a high-paying job, these people are living in financial ruin, servicing loans over the years to keep up with a wealthy lifestyle with nothing kept aside for retirement. You don't want to be in such a situation, do you? The first step to avoid getting roped into it is to prioritize your financial wellness immediately.

Financial wellness is the healthy management of your finances in a way that you are financially secure and able to live the kind of life that you've always wanted. Or at least the one you can comfortably afford. To be able to do this, you have to set financial goals and create plans on how to achieve those goals. Keep in mind that attaining financial wellness takes time, patience, and consistency. With those in mind, there are a few important things that you must factor into your financial plans while you head toward a healthier financial life.

Regularly evaluate your net worth. Many people tend to ignore this while riding the tides of life, having all the fun that they can get and drawing in liabilities and piling up debt along the way. On a regular basis (e.g., quarterly or annually), evaluate your net worth by taking account of all your assets and your liability. By subtracting your liabilities from assets, you can compute your net worth with ease. Doing this often helps you figure out what areas of your life need improving and budget accordingly.

Have plans in place. What financial plans do you have in place for yourself and your family? Those with high levels of financial wellness have laid out concrete plans for their finances. Though things don't usually go as we plan them, having backup plans can help you make up for some changes. Even when some changes come as a surprise, being flexible enough to pivot when needed can be a valuable skill. This could require you to make hard choices, to drop some seemingly pressing engagements for more reasonable ones. And as far as hard choices go, having clear priorities that are aligned with your values can help you make better financial decisions.

Don't ignore the need to build an emergency fund. It is important to have an emergency fund to cover expenses that are not planned for but must be met regardless. The rule of thumb for handling an emergency is to save up to six months equivalent to your living expenses. This way you will be able to survive without intense pressure for six months in the event that anything makes you incapable of working. I know that six months of living expenses might appear hefty, but you have to start somewhere. You might not be able to save up to six months' worth of living expenses, and that's perfectly fine. But you have to try to be disciplined enough not to spend what you are saving unless you have no other option. So, instead of stopping at Starbucks or checking into DoorDash, why not put that money aside to build up your emergency savings?

Protect and grow your finances. Because growth is constant, not growing your finances puts you at a disadvantage, with higher risks of elevated stress due to inflation. Not protecting the money you already have may be worse. You can consider working with a tax strategist or financial advisor to help you deal with tax issues and grow your money. Additionally, you can explore multiple streams of income. Depending entirely on one source of income can limit your financial growth potential. You can try out creative activities, considering that the internet has exposed creatives to opportunities beyond imagination.

Also keep an eye on your lifestyle inflation. As your career advances and promotions smile at you, your income is likely to increase. When this happens, there is a tendency that your expenses will climb too. You may spend more on wine to host a few new friends, buy some nice new suits to match your new Tesla, or eat out more because your work responsibilities increase and eating out appears to be a better use of your time. All these increased expenses are referred to as lifestyle inflation. Please take your time to review the changes you are making to your expenses to be sure that it's not simply to satisfy your desire to fit in.

Save. Save early. The earlier, the better. Because the importance of savings cannot be overemphasized. Saving up a percentage of your income is one of the most conservative ways to build wealth and avoid finance-related stress. Having a handsome amount of money put away gives you some level of psychological comfort, knowing that you are building toward a comfortable retirement. However, realizing this late can cause serious physical and mental strain. Starting early gives you enough time to build something reasonable before retirement. If the retirement age is sixty-five, for instance, you will have forty-three years to build up your financial fortress if you start when you are twenty-two. The same can't be said of another person that begins saving at the age of forty-seven.

To avoid finance-related stress, you should:

- Plan every bit of your finances.
- Pay yourself first by saving and investing first before spending.
- Set your priorities straight.
- Connect with finance experts (tax consultants, etc.) to get insights on how you can protect and grow your money.

Many Gen Xers and millennials are still grappling with the idea of retirement. According to a survey by CNBC, 61 percent of millennials plan to still get work engagements during retirement.[25] This may be because most older millennials do not have enough money put aside to fund a work-free retirement, and there's a reason why. Many millennials do not trust retirement plans and traditional investment vehicles that have served older generations during retirement. For one, the millennials' distrust of the stock market could be attributed to the fact that they have experienced multiple market crashes and more recessions than previous generations. In the United States alone, millennials have experienced up to ten stock market crashes and three recessions, along with two cryptocurrency market crashes. But finding ways to safeguard retirement today, despite the low trust for these financial markets, will help millennials and following generations build a more solid financial standing in the long future.

Protect your identity online. All it takes to bring your finances crashing down is your identity in the wrong hands. So, be aware of where you share your credit or debit card details, as well as any sensitive information that could enable con artists to impersonate you and make terrible financial decisions on your behalf.

PHYSICAL WELLNESS

It's hard to ignore the fact that physical fitness is the apparent image of a healthy life. That's what inspires most people to think that physical wellness is the ultimate way to build an absolutely healthy life. Our body is a reflection of how well we are inside. It is what we want others to see and how we want them to feel about us. Also, it is a visual representation of how we feel about ourselves. Most importantly, being physically well keeps you in great condition for optimum performance all around.

Not much else can be said about physical wellness and its relevance in our lives. It's the talk of every health-conscious person. They preach that we should eat healthily, exercise more, get adequate rest, and make appointments with the doctor routinely to keep track of our health and take precautionary measures when we're slipping off our wellness.

In simple terms, physical wellness is what we often refer to as healthy. It is the absence of medical and physical disease. It is the ability to stay up, move around, and perform without avoidable physical limitations. The steps to attaining physical wellness are not far from what you hear every day. However, its link with other pillars of wellness is not discussed enough. In the next chapter, The Wellness Loop, we will bring all the pillars of wellness together and see why we should treat them with a holistic approach. For now, I need you to know that it's neither too late nor too early to start making all areas of your wellness a priority.

Key Takeaways

1. Wellness is holistic, with eight pillars. Each pillar requires adequate attention at all times.

2. The starting point of your wellness journey is knowing yourself. Everything else is built upon it.

3. Your emotional (or psychological) well-being is the ultimate. The other seven pillars are designed to strengthen how you feel about yourself.

4. Everything is linked. Neglecting one is neglecting all.

CHAPTER THREE

The Wellness Wheel

During the *New York Times'* 2021 Dealbook Online Summit, world-renowned business leaders were interviewed about their views on the United States' business landscape. This interview got quite personal, and it doesn't take a genius to know that even these leaders with eleven-figure net worths have their regrets. For one, Adam Neumann, the founder of WeWork, expressed his regrets and failure of being aware of his company's financial wellness, forcing him to resign. The company went from $47 billion to $9 billion in valuation.[1] Any better reason to chalk up his regrets?

While Neumann's regret for his decision is normal and he could live with it for some reasons, not a lot of people have the ability to let things go and remain healthy. A simple regret can create an imbalance in your entire life if your wellness foundation is not rock solid. And the first step to creating a rock-solid wellness foundation is to understand the eight pillars discussed in the last chapter and treat them with a holistic approach.

Before I go on to explain what a holistic approach means, let me remind you of what each wellness pillar is about.

Emotional wellness reflects how well you understand and manage your feelings. Having a strong sense of self and expressing your emotions in productive ways is important for your emotional well-being. Productive ways to express emotions vary between people. For some, staying quiet or expressing themselves in subtle ways has always worked. For some people, letting off overwhelming emotions by screaming or hitting things has worked considerably well as well. Either way, you need to make sure that your expression does not hurt others in any way. So, if you have to, only scream and hit stuff in a controlled environment.

Spiritual wellness requires you to identify personal values that are aligned with your beliefs. Thereafter, use these values to define your purpose and goals. Staying connected to your core beliefs and a purpose that reinforces those beliefs helps you stay spiritually buoyant. Taking actions like forgiving yourself and others, creating life-guiding principles, and finding meaning in your life in ways that are selfless can help you improve your spiritual wellness.

Environmental wellness is your ability to take care of your immediate personal environment and take actions that will promote the sustainability of the global environment. Also, it requires you to identify, define, and live in a pleasant and adequately stimulating environment conducive to your growth and development as well as of those around you. Taking actions like recycling plastics, keeping your home clean and in healthy condition, and spending some time outdoors to connect with the environment and nature are important to your environmental well-being.

Social wellness describes your ability to build and be a part of a supportive social network. Connecting and engaging with others physically or virtually, nurturing healthy relationships, and supporting others are ways to improve your social wellness.

Intellectual wellness needs you to remain open-minded to new ideas, to actively seek knowledge, and engage in creative processes that challenge you to think critically and curiously. Committing your energy to self-development and setting clear learning goals within a topic will help you improve this pillar of wellness.

Occupational wellness is optimum when you find fulfillment in the work that you do. Choosing to pursue a profession or career that is aligned with your personal values and beliefs makes it easier to find self-fulfillment in your work. Your occupational wellness can greatly improve if you are able to find a balance between your work and personal life. Also, accurately estimating your professional capabilities and challenging yourself to improve will give you a sense of fulfillment as you work.

Financial wellness emphasizes your money management skills and your ability to live within your means in the moment and make realistic financial plans for your future in ways that allow you to live the life you've always wanted with minimal financial pressure.

> **Physical wellness** is what we often refer to as health. It requires you to maintain a healthy body by eating a healthy, balanced diet as well as exercising regularly. Developing a preventive lifestyle by always scheduling medical check-ups and having a healthy exercise routine are good ways to improve your physical well-being.

WELLNESS AND HEALTH

One common misconception happens when many people consider health and wellness as one and the same. While these two terms are closely related, they mean completely different things. To be healthy means being free from diseases and genetically okay. You can maintain a healthy life by regularly visiting the hospital, getting proper check-ups, eating healthy and balanced meals, and exercising regularly.

Wellness, on the other hand, is your ability to find balance in life. It includes living a healthy life, free from disease and more. Therefore, you could be healthy and unwell. You could be healthy, with all the biological markers and test results in the right range, yet going through difficulties in managing your professional career and relationships with the people you care about.

While you should make sure you focus on being healthy, you cannot afford to neglect other areas of your life. You have to design your environment for optimum productivity and creative freedom. Also, you need to engage in intellectual conversations to help you build your communication skills and refine your knowledge. All these may not be required to have a healthy life but are necessary to attain total wellness.

Since every part of your wellness is interconnected, it is up to you to find a balance in your life. This balance helps you keep all eight pillars of your wellness in equilibrium. While the healthy blood sugar and caffeine levels of every adult fall within a range, there is no numerical range used to estimate the balance in your life. However, you will know when you are living a balanced life because you will stress less. Even when you do, you derive a good sense of purpose from what you are doing, which makes you feel happy doing whatever you are doing.

You may be born healthy, with the perfect genetic composition and in an environment where creativity and cognitive development are enhanced. However, choosing to be completely well is a matter of choice. We are not predisposed to be well, given the rapid changes happening around us. We have to wake each day and choose wellness. And being able to achieve the sole purpose of finishing strong requires a holistic approach most of the time.

WHAT IS A HOLISTIC APPROACH TO WELLNESS?

Simply referred to as holistic wellness, this approach needs you to look at yourself as one being with multiple sections. Each of these sections is interconnected in a way that leaving one in bad condition will affect the functionality of the others. The effect one has on others may vary depending on the individual.

Therefore, you have to view all eight pillars of wellness (discussed in the previous chapter) as connected parts of your complete well-being, giving each the proper attention. Neglecting your physical well-being by failing to exercise or eat healthily may lead to conditions like obesity and cardiovascular diseases. These diseases, in turn, can hinder your ability to function in the workplace (occupational), socialize with others around you (social), create a terrible sense of self (mental), and limit your engagement in intellectual debates.

On the other hand, focusing entirely on your physical fitness with very little or no attention to your financial well-being might create a situation where you saddle yourself with debt by purchasing the latest fitness gear. This could lead to emotional stress when other important things require your financial commitment (e.g., family expenses and college education). In summary, you must find a balance. In this chapter, I will walk you through the first step of finding balance: identifying the balance point. It is almost impossible to successfully search for something you cannot recognize. So, we will first learn to assess our balance using the Wellness Wheel. A properly assessed Wellness Wheel can help you live a well-rounded life.

WHAT DOES IT MEAN TO LIVE A WELL-ROUNDED LIFE?

Let me stimulate your imagination briefly. Can you imagine yourself as a socially outgoing person with a moderate number of exciting and intelligent friends that truly value you? Imagine that you really do engage in smart debates with these amazing friends of yours, and you talk about philosophy, politics, sports, science, global economies, and finance. At work, your boss finds you favorable and is preparing for a promotion. Is that exciting to think about?

On a cold Saturday evening, after having been out with some friends, you return home to a neighborhood with green trees and fresh air, serene, with really cool kids playing around the court, cheerful and carefree. Your apartment is neatly structured, the central heat is in perfect condition, and your bills are well covered. You just wired a few hundred bucks to your niece in college to cover her living expenses for the coming week. Now, you are lying back after picking up a book from the shelf behind the sidebar to read. Does it look perfect? Does it feel like the life you want to have?

Well, that is what it feels like to be well-rounded. To have the right mix of skills, knowledge, and capabilities required to perform optimally in all eight areas of your life. This means that you are environmentally aware enough to live in a peaceful neighborhood and model your apartment to inspire healthy habits. Your social network consists of smart friends who engage in healthy debates about topics that really matter and motivate you to learn more. Your career is on the right path, and you are happy with the work that you are doing while you are also well connected with your beliefs.

Even though this sounds like a movie script or an avatar of your perfect life, you have to know that it is very possible for someone to have such a well-rounded life. And you, too, can have it. As a matter of fact, nobody deserves a well-rounded life more than you do. Nevertheless, you should not mistake a well-rounded for a perfect life.

Being well-rounded is far from being perfect and above life. Nobody is above life. We all go through life-related stress and constant changes in our environment. A really dear friend may get transferred, or you might have a not-so-good day at work. Whatever it is, you should know that it won't always be rosy. Well-rounded people understand this and live accordingly. They know that unexpected events will happen and that they have to adapt, change, or cope. They can avoid things that swing their emotions to extremes and make sure they don't greatly impact their relationships with other people and their environment.

From time to time, it's a very human experience to slip and let emotions get the better of you. What matters is that you work hard day by day to make sure that you're building your coping mechanisms and strategies so that the next time, your response might not be the same and, in fact, might keep you from slipping. Being well-rounded helps you make sure this doesn't happen too often. But how do you become well-rounded?

It may seem more manageable for you to focus on building up one of the wellness pillars (let's say intellectual) before moving on to the next pillar (let's say social) and work each of them out in that manner. Approaching these pillars individually will keep you off balance for a long time. One of the reasons is that each pillar is boundless. You can't reach the peak of intelligence, nor can you be social enough, spiritual enough, eco-friendly enough or even fit enough. Following a holistic approach to build up your wellness muscles is a better and more potent idea. What this means is that in order for you to feel completely well, you need to create a plan to simultaneously work on each pillar in unison.

> A well-rounded person:
>
> - Has a good sense of self and is attuned with their emotions.
> - Appreciates the environment and consciously engages in activities that are environmentally friendly.
> - Makes efforts to build a supportive social network.
> - Is curious, actively seeks knowledge, and engages in creative activities.
> - Plans finances carefully, spends responsibly, and protects their money.
> - Believes in, engages with, and supports a selfless spiritual cause.
> - Regularly participates in physical activities that keep the body functional.
> - Has a career that they are passionate about and is aligned with their purpose.

Our wellness goals vary. Some may be more inclined toward spirituality, while others are enthusiastic about cognitive intelligence. Find the amount of time and effort to commit to each wellness activity in a way that your stronger values are getting enough attention without having other areas suffer neglect. You can find the exact balance that works for you by using the Wellness Wheel.

THE WELLNESS WHEEL

In 1948, the World Health Organization first defined wellness as a state of complete physical, mental, and social well-being beyond the mere absence of disease. This was the awakening moment in the study of human wellness. Eleven years later, Dr. Halbert Dunn published a paper that further explained complete wellness. In his 1959 paper, he proposed that complete wellness is not simply the state of being sound in mind and body. It is an ever-changing perspective of life that arises as you explore the changes happening around you.

To maintain balance as these changes happen must be a conscious choice that we all make every day. Since changes can be rapid at times while subtle at others, it's difficult to always stay balanced. In his paper, Dr. Dunn proposed a wellness grid that paired our health (social, mental, and physical) against the environment that we find ourselves in. According to Dr. Dunn's model of assessing wellness, living in a poor environment with a below-average health condition is a terrible state to be in. Moving to a more favorable environment with similar conditions is merely protecting your poor health from escalating. Sound health, on the other hand, may be hindered by a poor environment.

So, at that time, people were encouraged to always strive to be in good health and to live in a favorable environment.

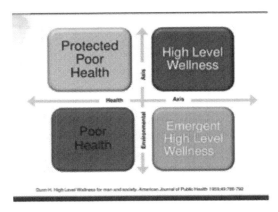

As studies around wellness advanced, the pillars of wellness emerged. In 1976, Dr. Bill Hettler developed the Wellness Wheel. At the time, it brought all six known pillars of wellness into perspective and allowed people to match their activities with each pillar.

Today, as our world has continued to get more complex, other pillars of wellness have emerged and have become very important parts of our lives. Added to Dr. Hettler's pillars were financial and environmental wellness. However, some people may add more pillars or substitute some to fit their wellness goals. For instance, retired seniors who have beautiful careers and healthy retirement plans may not consider including financial and occupational wellness in their priorities. Depending on their values, they may include cultural wellness or simply work with a six-pillar Wellness Wheel.

For many millennials and Gen Zers whose finances and occupations are the center of their adult lives, using an eight-pillar Wellness Wheel is ideal since it brings all the areas of life into perspective. This is what the eight-pillar Wellness Wheel looks like.

▌ ASSESSING YOUR WELLNESS WITH THE WHEEL

Finding a balance on the Wellness Wheel varies from one person to another. This means everyone is responsible for finding their own balance. Knowing how to use the Wellness Wheel can help you identify your own balance and thread the needle comfortably.

You should keep in mind that your balance point changes frequently. Every time you assess your life using the Wellness Wheel, you may discover a new balance point that you should try to maintain for optimal wellness. Maintaining complete wellness is more of an art than a science, and knowing how to find balance is crucial to perfecting that art.

You should also remember that measuring your life against the Wellness Wheel every day may not be a good idea. This could be overwhelming, considering you need time to work, exercise, and keep your life going. Always give yourself some time to adapt to the major changes happening around you. Making time to take the wellness assessment every month is a really positive practice to incorporate into your calendar. Nevertheless, you should consider creating daily checklists of activities that can help you achieve your wellness goals. Engaging in these activities and returning to your Wellness Wheel periodically to assess their impact can help you find balance over time.

Now, when focusing on finding a balance, this framework will be helpful.

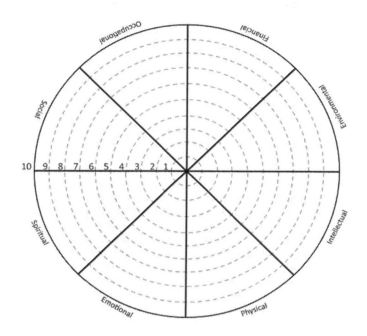

Using this framework, you can rate your level of well-being for each pillar on a scale of ten. You should take time to be alone for deep reflection. You will review your current life in every area and rate it accordingly on the Wellness Wheel.

To make it easier to measure the strength of each wellness pillar, you can create a list of five or ten questions for each pillar. These questions will carry equal significance to the well-being being assessed. Here are a few examples to consider. However, ensure to create your own, as everyone's values are unique.

SOCIAL

QUESTIONS	ANSWER	SCORE
1. Did you attend a social event this week?		
2. Did you make a new friend this week?		
3. Have you expressed support to any friend this week?		
4. Did you check on, visit, or send gifts to any of your friends or colleagues this week?		
5. Did you receive a gift, visit, or check-up call from any friend or colleague this week?		
TOTAL SCORE		

SPIRITUAL

QUESTIONS	ANSWER	SCORE
1. Did you meditate daily throughout this week?		
2. Did you go out to appreciate nature?		
3. Did you make any donations this week?		
4. Did you go to your place of worship this week?		
5. Did you live according to your beliefs and values?		
6. Did you express gratitude to the people that crossed your path this week?		
7. Did you connect with your inner self to find out what you really need to stay happy this week?		
TOTAL SCORE		

EMOTIONAL

QUESTIONS	ANSWER	SCORE
1. Were you cheerful most of the week?		
2. Did you express your feelings to others in ways that are not hurtful?		
3. Did you adapt well to the changes around you?		
4. Did you write down your reactions toward the changes happening around you?		
5. Did you identify the particular change that triggered you or made you feel upset?		
6. Do you feel happy with yourself?		
7. Are you feeling anxious about something?		
TOTAL SCORE		

PHYSICAL

QUESTIONS	ANSWER	SCORE
1. Did you work out three times this week?		
2. Did you drink up to three liters of water daily throughout this week?		
3. Did you check your blood sugar levels this week?		
4. Did you check your blood pressure this week?		
5. Was your caffeine consumption within healthy limits this week?		

6. Did you do some stretching this week to keep yourself from feeling stiff?		
TOTAL SCORE		

INTELLECTUAL

QUESTIONS	ANSWER	SCORE
1. Did you read a book this week?		
2. Did you complete any creative tasks this week?		
3. Did you engage in any healthy debates with a friend this week?		
4. Did you solve any critical thinking puzzles this week?		
5. Did you learn something new this week?		
TOTAL SCORE		

ENVIRONMENTAL

QUESTIONS	ANSWER	SCORE
1. Did you recycle the plastics you used this week?		
2. Did you clean your apartment this week?		
3. Did you plant or water a tree this week?		
4. Did you buy or use a product that is eco-friendly this week?		
5. Was the noise level in your home environment within healthy limits this week?		

6. Are there distractions in/around your home office keeping you from being productive?		
TOTAL SCORE		

FINANCIAL

QUESTIONS	ANSWER	SCORE
1. Did you save any money toward retirement this week?		
2. Did you make any impulse purchases this week?		
3. Have you planned out your expenses for next week?		
4. Are your expenses this week below your means?		
TOTAL SCORE		

OCCUPATIONAL

QUESTIONS	ANSWER	SCORE
1. Did you have good relationships with your colleagues this week?		
2. Were your bosses pleased with your performance this week?		
3. Did you take enough personal time from work this week?		
4. Did you meet your expectations at work this week?		
5. Have you worked on a development plan to move you to the next phase in your career?		

6. Did you chat with your managers this week to get clear on the opportunities available for you?		
7. Are you coping well with the pressures at work?		
TOTAL SCORE		

The assessment tables should be used alongside the Wellness Wheel, which is calibrated on a scale of 1–10. The calibrations are shown as small circles inside the large wheel. Each of the questions above should carry equal score points. If the answer to any of the questions above positively impacts your wellness, you can award it a score of 10 points. Do not award any point for an answer to a question that has a negative impact. To explain further, learning something new each week is good for your intellectual well-being. So, if the answer to the *"Did you learn anything new thing this week?"* question is "Yes," you can award it a full point.

After answering all of the questions, you can add the points on each assessment table to give the "Total Score." Find the average of the total score so that it fits into the 1–10 scale. Then return to the Wellness Wheel and mark the appropriate circle. This will help you discover what area of your life needs more attention in the coming week. For instance, if your financial wellness score averages eight points while your environmental wellness score averages three points, you should increase your consciousness toward the effect of your actions on the environment. You have to spend the next month tuning down the sound level in your personal environment, buying more eco-friendly alternatives, and several other environmentally friendly activities.

Also, maintaining a worksheet to keep track of your development over time will be really helpful. By using the worksheet, you can see how far you have come in your wellness journey. There is a sense of accomplishment that comes from measurable growth.

IMPORTANT: Don't forget to create assessment questions that are aligned with your personal wellness goals, values, and principles. The tables above are merely examples to aid comprehension, although you could also use them as a source of inspiration to create your own.

WELLNESS FEEDBACK LOOP

Your wellness journey is a continuous learning process. The lessons learned from each wellness activity that you engage in are used to reinforce or correct the practice. For example, if you attended four social events in the month and find that you haven't made any genuine friendships with whom you share similar beliefs and values, you may consider choosing your social events with more care or reassess your values to better suit your personality and wellness goals. This phenomenon of improving your activities based on the result of previous efforts is called the **feedback loop**.

When you use the Wellness Wheel to assess your various levels of well-being, it will guide your reflections and awareness toward different areas of your life. Referring to the "social table" above, it is important to send gifts, make check-up calls to your friends and colleagues, and ensure you take COVID safety measures when you pay a visit to your friends. However, if none of these efforts are reciprocated (that is, if you are not receiving check-up calls, gifts, and visitations), you may take some time to reflect on the reason why people aren't returning the energy that you give to them.

Trying to find out what is wrong will help you understand whether you are with the right friends or not. They may value you but do not have the resources or the time to return the gestures because they are out of a job or too busy with some serious personal challenges. Or, as much as we hate to accept this, they may simply be uninterested in having you in their social network. Whichever the case, using the feedback loop to channel your energy properly can help you maintain balance in the long run.

Investing your energy in people who are happy to have you as a friend (or acquaintance) can make a great difference. When you give positive energy, you are more likely to receive positive energy in return. This happens in your social life and all other areas. A positive attitude toward work, life, and friendship is important if you want to achieve positive results. Emotionally, expressing more gratitude, laughing more, and positively adapting to changes all have a direct impact on your life. Through self-reflection, you will recognize these impacts and adjust your emotional practices accordingly.

▌DEVELOPING YOUR OWN CYCLE OF WELLNESS

As was previously mentioned, wellness is a journey. It is an interesting and endless stream of adventure. You are constantly exploring your capabilities and riding the waves of this shoreless ocean called life. With every ride you take, when the tide calms down at sunset, you should take a moment to reflect on your activities during the day and plan for the next day. And when the sun rises, you will show up and try to do better. Your wellness journey should be approached with similar levels of excitement and commitment. To be able to do this, you need to bring yourself into the wellness cycle.

Reflect on your general well-being. It is the first step to take to help you find balance in life. You need to settle down to discover how you are feeling within yourself and what is making you feel that way. Are you stressed and overwhelmed? Are you having trouble sleeping? Are you having a hard time focusing on a single task because too much is happening around you at the same time? Whatever it is, you need to step back for a moment to identify and clearly define it.

Put together a plan of action. After some reflection, you will have a few suspicions as to why you are facing distress in some areas of your life. Take the time to create a plan that, when implemented, could stop the distress, either by eliminating the cause or changing how you respond to it. I advise you to write this plan down to serve as a point of reference. Also, writing your plan down helps your brain engage fully in your thought process and refine the plan to work.

Implement your plans. Simply putting plans on paper won't make your intentions happen. You have to consciously take actions that are in accordance with your laid-out plan. Remember, only actions produce results. Not talks or plans. However, acting without planning is dangerous.

Review your performance. Take a moment to look at how much of a difference your actions made. Did they change anything? Were the changes what you anticipated? How much impact did your actions make, and where were they most impactful? After reviewing the results of your actions, you can begin the cycle again by reflecting on your well-being and discovering how it can be improved.

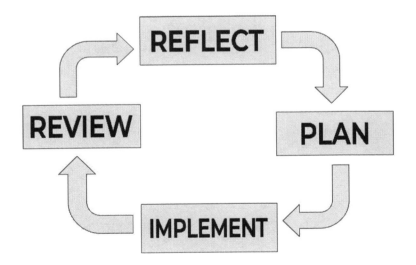

Our well-being is our responsibility, and we must guard it with all seriousness. Actively assessing our current levels of wellness using the Wellness Wheel is a viable way to find and maintain balance throughout our lives. Nevertheless, as we (humans) are not isolated beings, our environment, friends, and the organizations that we work with have vital roles to play in our wellness journey. In the next chapter, Sharing the Chores, I will explain the roles that employers and friends have to play in our wellness journey. Also, you will clearly learn what responsibilities are solely reserved for you as you seek wellness for yourself and those around you.

Key Takeaways

1. The process of attaining wellness is ever evolving. You have to continuously find your balance as life's events unfold.

2. The Wellness Wheel opens your eyes to the area(s) of your wellness journey that needs special attention while keeping other areas out of your scope.

3. Using the Wellness Wheel to assess your wellness monthly can help you find and maintain balance.

4. Everybody's wellness journey is unique. To successfully find your balance, you should create an assessment that is unique to you.

PART TWO

Attaining Total Wellness

CHAPTER FOUR

Sharing the Chores

In typical shared spaces, there are always staff members that rest all of their wellness responsibilities on their employers, the HR/People Operations department, or their direct managers. They show up to work every day anticipating that their manager is going to be in a bright mood. Their moods swing south upon reprimands, but they are seldom elated when praised for their contribution to the team. They want to do great work and be productive, happy, and excited about working. Yet none of these are happening. They pin their hopes on promotions and salary raises, believing that one of these could make them happier and more fulfilled at work. Unfortunately, neither will help when they eventually come.

As the slow fingers of time creep along, frustration builds up within them. They gradually become more of a burden to themselves and the people around them because of downward social and occupational spirals spurred by negative emotions. Sooner or later, they begin to see work as a dreaded part of their lives that helps pay the bills, a necessary evil. In the real sense, doing work that we love and care about gives us a sense of purpose and makes life worth living.

It is not entirely up to your HR/People Operations Team, manager, or even organizational leadership to make work enjoyable. Sure, they have a responsibility to take appropriate measures to keep their team clear on goals/ objectives, motivated, and thriving. But it's up to you to find what connects closely to your purpose in the work that you do. That is the one way to find fulfillment in your professional life.

> You are responsible for 70–80 percent of your wellness. The organizations that you work for and your social network can collectively make up for the rest.

It gets a tad troubling when challenges from work affect the prosperity of our relationships with others outside of shared professional spaces. Some people are socially awkward such that being around them just makes you feel down for no reason. Some people call it bad vibes. These people may not always socialize as much as their peers. But you can't entirely blame them for not being outgoing because it appears that they could use some help.

While your social network, professional colleagues, and employer have significant roles to play in helping you become a well-rounded person, you are ultimately responsible for most of this work. You need to identify your responsibilities in relation to your wellness, as well as those of your friends and colleagues. Thus, you can act accordingly to build a mutually beneficial social network and fulfilling professional career. The objective of this chapter is to help you understand what your responsibilities are while spelling out what you should expect from your social network and how you can leverage the support of your employer to achieve total wellness. If you follow through to the end of this chapter, you will understand how to share your wellness chores and play your part successfully.

ORGANIZATIONS HAVE THEIR RESPONSIBILITIES

Some of the top organizations are prioritizing staff wellness. They are taking measures to ensure that their staff are performing at their best. And that's one of the smartest ideas that the global workforce has implemented because when people are happy and well, they are more productive.

Considering that work takes center stage in our lives as millennials and Gen Zers, not loving the work that you do is no better than torture. Great managers and organizational leaders know this, and they are setting the groundwork to make sure everyone is well taken care of. Nevertheless, there is a limit to what they can do for you.

Your physical fitness may be your sole responsibility, but many organizations are helping their staff shoulder the cost of keeping the physical pillar standing upright. Several organizations now offer their staff free gym memberships to help them stay fit. Mental health stipends are now a thing in organizations that make staff wellness a priority. Although it may not be a very attractive thing for those that are picky with food, some organizations are even providing healthy meals or meal boxes for their teams to ensure that they have one less decision to make on any given week and that they are able to break bread with those they care about. But how about rest?

It's easy to think that an organization that offers all these wellness benefits will have the urge to work you until you burn out. Well, they don't. Netflix, LinkedIn, and Virgin Groups (to name three) give their staff unlimited vacation, allowing staff to take the time to rest and return to work refreshed and happy. Some organizations ensure that their staff take these vacations at a particular time of the year. This is because people are likely to put off the need to focus on their wellness for a later time, which in my experience, almost never arrives. But if all organizations are doing is caring for your physical well-being, how about your finances?

Your finances are very personal to you. You don't want to let people know that you are saving up for a new car or how much you save monthly. Neither would you think it cool to disclose how much of a mortgage repayment you are shouldering each month. Great organizations are making the effort to see that this wellness pillar is standing strong in the lives of their staff. Some provide financial initiatives to educate their staff about how to build a stronger financial wellness pillar. Beyond this education, organizations have to take important actions to secure the finances of staff. The Revenue Act of 1978 that created the 401k in the United States has, over time, come to be one of the best ways of providing for the future financial needs of staff members.[1] And this is the bare minimum that an organization should offer today. In recent times, many organizations are taking these financial initiatives particularly seriously because finance-related stress can cripple productivity just as much as any other emotional challenge.

Regarding emotional wellness, there's much done. The best organizations are doing their best to help staff members find a balance. Despite all of the benefits that come with working in wonderful organizations, the demand to perform coupled with the challenges of personal life can be distressing. Organizations are catering to the mental wellness of their team as well. So, if you are working with a great organization, there are chances that your emotional well-being is on their plate and something they are considering. Big organizations with resources have on-site yoga studios where meditation classes are offered. This is to help you build a better connection with yourself, define your true values, and explore your chances at self-fulfillment in the organization for which you're working.

However, there is no one-size-fits-all wellness approach. Our emotional compositions and needs vary. In a diverse organization, our environmental, spiritual, and social beliefs and values differ. These differences affect our wellness needs. Furthermore, wellness priorities are not the same for you and the colleague whom you are closest to. A colleague may be concerned about looking forty when she is near the retirement age of sixty-five, while another colleague is looking to actually retire at forty. The former goal requires prioritizing physical well-being while the latter focuses on the financial aspect. Whatever the individual goals of staff members are, there are ways that organizations can help them achieve them.

The first step to making it possible for everyone is to create a culture that allows people to freely talk about their wellness challenges. To make this possible, they should seek counsel from appropriate individuals within the organization like the People Operations team. Organizations can begin by creating wellness programs with the sole objective of promoting wellness in their various shared spaces. Educating people about their wellness responsibilities and the resources that the organization has made available to them can help set the foundations for a more productive work culture.

However, the responsibility for creating and facilitating wellness programs in various organizations has been tossed around between departments and different levels of leadership. Who should spearhead the promotion of a wellness culture? Which staff should be at the forefront of this program?

Because it is the responsibility of everyone, some organizations leave it to their staff to figure out what works best for them. In other cases, it is the HR/People Operations team that is tasked with ensuring that the organization's well-being is prioritized and that staff productivity is good. Nonetheless, as our wellness needs are unique, creating organization-wide wellness is very taxing for HR/People Operations departments, especially in big organizations.

In that case, several small committees can be created to help reach more staff. These committees will consist of staff and leaders with sound knowledge of general human wellness. They should execute organization-wide wellness goals approved by leadership to ensure that everyone is working under the best possible conditions. What happens when there are disconnects in wellness knowledge among staff members?

Third-party wellness experts can be brought in to create and organize wellness programs and help the organization set realistic wellness goals, as well as create a road map to achieving those goals. Most times, bringing in external wellness experts can be revealing. They may not know staff members on a personal level and will not be at the organization longer than they should. Sometimes these people make it easier for the staff to freely express their challenges. Another reason is their experience in helping people gain the confidence required to solve wellness problems. They can see through your challenges by simply asking the right questions and assessing the right performance metrics. It is what they do, and the right experts are good at it.

Despite these possibilities though, not many of these organizations effectively implement wellness programs. Inasmuch as many would like to play a role in improving staff well-being, several challenges hold them back.

Scheduling inflexibility as a result of high workloads is one of the primary challenges that organizations face, especially big ones.[2] While wellness programs are great for the progress of the organization, they can't afford to run them at the expense of corporate activities. And in a typical workplace, there is a lot to be done with little time to spare for several wellness meetings. And even though wellness meetings are a part of the organization's culture, getting a free forty-five minutes out of everyone's calendar at exactly the same time is almost impossible. A lot of people have to make trade-offs to attend these meetings, and who knows how long they can continue to make those trades.

The emotional energy required to discuss wellness challenges with colleagues is another reason why organizations aren't excelling in their wellness pursuits. This energy demand is higher for leaders, who may find it out of place to discuss their wellness needs and challenges with direct reports or junior staff.

WELLNESS IN MODERN SHARED SPACES

Before the pandemic, many organizations weren't treating staff wellness as a top priority. As the pandemic struck and nonessential workers were forced to work remotely, organizations shifted their focus to how they could help their staff maintain balance. Our social lives as humans were stripped from us, and our wellness was threatened. Human connection took a big hit. For some, deprivation from socializing caused all their well-being to come crashing down like dominoes. Our financial well-being took a hit as people started shopping online impulsively, most of which wouldn't have been considered before now.[3] Many people lost their jobs. One hundred and forty-four million Americans lost their jobs during that time, causing a serious strain on their occupational well-being. To make ends meet, many were forced to take on odd jobs that were not aligned with their personal values and beliefs.[4] Many of these decisions were driven by the need to financially support their extended family and friends. Some others had to step back to take care of sick loved ones.

Physically, the lockdown caused a lot of people to gain weight. In the UK, 40 percent of adults gained weight during that time.[5] In the US, adults gained two pounds of weight for every month throughout the lockdown.[6] Many people developed poor eating habits, and not much changed in the rate of exercise to compensate for the increased eating frequency among adults.[7] Many people paid more attention to their hygiene during this time, but that wasn't chiefly because they willingly sought hygiene improvements. The emotional distress from watching pandemic guidance from news outlets sent shivers of fear down the spines of many. So, improving hygiene was a precautionary measure encouraged by the CDC and many other health organizations. Furthermore, our lack of social engagements, financial and productivity downslide, among many other things, caused serious mental health issues. During these times, great organizations played their role. They did so impressively well, I might add.

Organizations took their corporate social responsibilities more seriously during this time to help their staff get through the challenging phase. Many people reported their wellness needs being well cared for by their employers despite the high probability of layoffs, which contributed to people's anxiety. As everyone worked in virtual shared spaces during this time, they were drawn apart from each other and closer to themselves. And despite the efforts of these organizations, staff members' satisfaction at work and loyalty to the organizations that they worked for did not improve.[8] In fact, it went the opposite way. Why?

Organizations can only do so much to help you achieve total wellness. You have far more to do for yourself than anyone can do for you.

▌LARGER IS YOUR COURT

Nobody understands you like you do. And truthfully, nobody ever will. Not your therapist, parents, siblings, or your closest friends. These people can only define you based on the information at their disposal. That is, they only know what they see or perceive about you. And this information is too limited to define your source of happiness. Too many people are stuck between defining themselves and accepting the public's perceived definition of them. And sadly, this has caused more emotional distress than imaginable. Out of the over eight hundred thousand suicides that happen each year, a significant percentage is inspired by the high expectation placed on Gen Zers and millennials by society.[9] You don't have to allow society to dictate your identity, personal beliefs, values, and principles. You alone are responsible for identifying and defining yourself in ways that are aligned with your well-being and personality. Without first accomplishing this, you are probably just existing. The next chapter will enlighten you on how to start living instead of merely existing. But first, you need to recognize your responsibility in the quest to find and maintain balance in life.

Most of your responsibilities rely on your ability to define your personality. Knowing how you are different from those around you can help you connect with them better. There are several types of human personalities, each of which has its own unique strengths and weaknesses. Defining your personality allows you to identify the positive traits that you possess and how you can use them to live the life that you really want. While you may be glad that you have amazing positive traits, there are negative attributes that you might not be particularly proud of having. You do not need to feel bad for having them. We are all a combination of positive and negative energies, and our responsibility is to balance them and ensure that the positive ones are expressed more. So, the first step to improving or controlling the influence of these not-so-good traits in your life is to **identify them**.

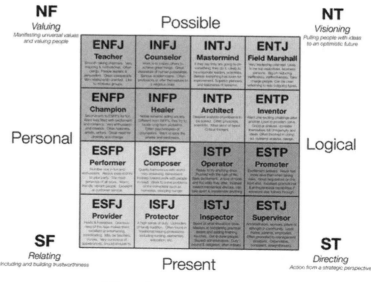

©Myers-Briggs Personality Types

Do you get uncontrollably angry sometimes? Do you get anxious when you are praised publicly? By identifying these personality traits, you can start identifying the things that really make you angry and how you can avoid them or build up your tolerance. If public praise upsets you, you can always share with your manager how you feel and offer suggestions for better ways to deliver high fives.

Another major responsibility that you must bear on your own is the burden of self-discipline. You probably know that eating healthy meals is important to your well-being, as well as exercising regularly and drinking moderately. And even though your organization offers the interesting wellness benefits that are discussed above, it is entirely up to you to get up every day and work out. Nobody should have to pull you up to attend yoga classes. Restaurants will always serve dessert, but consuming it is your decision. So, without disciplining yourself to do the right things required for achieving your wellness goals, all the efforts from your social network, colleagues, and the organization you work for would not make a big difference.

The ability to discipline yourself is not easy, especially when no one is watching or there to hold you accountable. However, there are several tricks that you can use to make the fight less frustrating. Redesigning your environment and leaving cues can help you stay committed to performing activities that will enhance your wellness. James Clear, in his book *Atomic Habits*, explained the importance of environmental cues in cultivating new habits. Instead of keeping soda in your refrigerator, fill it up with bottles of water. Keep a big bowl of fruit on the kitchen counter or dining table. You are very likely to pick some up whenever you walk into the kitchen or dining. Keep a clean gym kit in the car whenever you are going to work. It's easier for you to stop by at the gym on your way back than to go back to the gym after getting home. All these things can help make self-discipline more spontaneous.

An appropriately redesigned environment shouldn't focus only on facilitating desired habits. Hygiene and creative stimulation should also be considered. Regardless of your personality type, your immediate environment should be clean and habitable, as well as free from disease-causing pests. Then, considering your personality type, you should put stimulating cues around your environment to spark creative thinking. Some people are keen on perfection; therefore, they may want the position of their furniture to be precise. Other people may derive a constant sense of satisfaction and self-worth from looking at their creations. If you are this type of person, you should consider creating some artwork and a few Do-It-Yourself (DIY) furniture projects and keeping them around the home to improve your mood and help put a smile on your face from time to time.

While your personal environment is a reflection of you, treating the outer environment appropriately is a sign of care for others and for our lovely planet. Using eco-friendly products, servicing your fuel-powered vehicles regularly to minimize carbon emissions, and taking action to improve the planet's green life are ways of enhancing the global environment. And as the world tries to help Earth heal from the ruin brought by human civilization, your efforts will go a long way toward making positive changes. Don't hold back on it!

In striving to promote good environmental policies, your life's purpose shouldn't be neglected. Remember, no one can choose it for you. You are responsible for taking all the experiences that life has given you and using them to carve out a purpose for yourself. What is your experience? Did you grow up in a low socioeconomic neighborhood where the rate of college admission was low among adolescents? Were too many young men in your neighborhood getting hooked on crime and drug use? Have you discovered that your genetic origin has been traced to a remote region in Africa where clean water and basic medical supplies are insufficient?

Whatever it is, you need to take it in and carve a purpose for yourself. This purpose helps you create goals to pursue, choose the most appropriate career, and build effective strategies for achieving these goals. It gives you a reason to remain alive. According to a 2019 study by JAMA Network, people with a well-defined purpose live longer and happier than those who fail to define their purpose.[10] Fortunately, no one is in a better position to define your purpose than you are.

Finding purpose is one thing; achieving it is another. It can be emotionally draining to have defined your purpose but not have figured out how to pursue it. Seeking the required help is up to you. No matter who you speak to, until you meet the right people who understand the message you carry, it is almost impossible to make a difference. You need to actively seek out mentors and coaches that can guide you. Great coaches and mentors know their strengths and will be honest with you. They will respect you enough to let you know when your demands are outside their scope of understanding and recommend a more suitable mentor or coach to the best of their knowledge. But you have to make the move, because they may not come to find you.

> Knowing your personality type helps you find productive ways to pursue your life's purpose. You can start by taking online personality assessment tests.

Meeting the one mentor that will make the difference may not be easy, but you have to always try. And in most cases, you will combine the knowledge and counsel of more than one mentor, who are experts in different areas. Either way, keep in mind that great mentors seldom focus on your career advancements. Instead, they will always focus on helping you grow as a person.[11] That way, they can advise you to put yourself above your career whenever you are at a crossroads. Also, it's best to find a mentor with whom you share similar values and aligned purposes.

Lastly, but no less importantly, your associations matter, and choosing them is your sole responsibility. The people you surround yourself with can influence your life more than you could ever imagine. Be cautious about choosing friends. Focus on building personal relationships with people who are conscious of their well-being and are focused on finding and maintaining balance. Remember that hanging around smokers, for instance, not only increases your chances of trying out cigarettes and getting hooked but also increases your risk of developing and dying from heart disease.[12] And sadly, the chances are higher if you don't smoke but hang around smokers.

This doesn't mean that you have to be mean to the friends you once had and don't want to be around anymore. You can gently advise them and explain why they need to prioritize their wellness as well as the need to find and maintain balance in their lives. Always repeating this advice at every given opportunity may force them to adhere to it or simply create a gap between you and them. So, the relationship may eventually wither without serious opposition. If your social network does matter so much to your wellness, what role do they play in helping you find and maintain balance?

THE SOCIAL CATALYSTS

Did you know that an obsessed person is more likely to have a friend or friend of a friend that is obsessed? Well, evidence cited by American sociologist Nicholas Christakis revealed this fact.[13] Our wellness is subjective. This means that it is influenced by our personal opinions and feelings. And these opinions and feelings are influenced by the people we associate with. If we feel and opine that safely visiting the gym, working out at home, or taking a run are a conscious waste of productive hours, we are likely to communicate this notion to our friends and family, finding ways to make our argument in convincing ways. This is how our opinions and feelings are influenced by the people we hold in high esteem and listen to.

Also, there are many points of influence that affect our well-being, including marriage, friendship, workplace, and neighborhood ties. All of these are "robustly related to life satisfaction and happiness."[14] Invariably, our social network does have a role to play in our ability to find and maintain balance in life. What are these roles?

Your social network is a buffer from negative events. When bad things in life happen and we take unexpected hits, recovery is faster when we have amazing friends, neighbors, and family to connect with, either remotely or in person. Their presence and, in many cases, their sense of humor allow healing to happen faster. Therefore, it is the responsibility of your social group to offer their support to you when you are going through a rough moment. Don't forget that you owe the same responsibility to your friends, neighbors, and family because to whom support is given, support is expected.

Opportunities do not announce themselves, at least not to everyone that needs them. And the information that could bring these opportunities to you at the times when you need them is propagated through other people. The people around you can notify you of new job openings in case you are considering a new career, a career change, or provide recommendations when you wish to see a therapist for the first time. Regardless of your needs, it's always great to speak to someone, and these people are your first points of contact.

Although it is believed that our network owes us support, it is selfish to feel entitled to it. You need to always consider the possibility that someone within your network is also dealing with personal challenges and has to prioritize themselves at that moment. For that reason, they may be unavailable to provide the support that you need. However, it is crucial that you communicate with them to create an avenue to discuss the challenges that you are facing and review if you might help each other.

Amazing organizations, wonderful friends, strong coping skills, and good personal accountability measures are a good recipe for finding balance in life and pursuing your total wellness goals. Their impacts on our lives are highly valued, and there is very little we can do without them. However, we have an even greater responsibility to ourselves. Until those responsibilities are met, the efforts of our friends, family, neighbors, colleagues, and managers may be pointless. In the next chapter, you will learn the essential steps to achieving total wellness and becoming a well-rounded person.

Key Takeaways

1. Even though most great organizations are doing their best to help staff members maintain balance, you are responsible for finding your unique balance, taking the required actions to maintain that balance, and making plans for your future.

2. Work takes center stage in our lives. You should love what you do or consider finding something that you love and engaging in it.

3. To choose a career with a better chance of satisfaction and happiness, you should start by identifying your personality type.

4. The well-being of your social network will probably rub off on you. Encourage your friends to prioritize their wellness or consider finding and connecting with the people that already do.

CHAPTER FIVE

5 Steps to Complete Wellness

Despite advancements in technology and health care, the sad reality that besets us is that we, millennials, and Gen Zers are in a fairly poor position in regards to wellness. According to a study by JAMA Network, only 5 percent of millennials are getting enough sleep and engaging in adequate physical activity.[1] That leaves 95 percent of a young population at high risk of physical and emotional unwellness.

More than any other generation, millennials are spending more hours working, and while some struggle with sleep, others are spending more time sleeping than older generations. This is leaving many people with significantly less time to dedicate to their social, financial, and intellectual well-being. Unfortunately, you can't blame them entirely for devoting too much to their occupation. With crippling student loans hanging over the head of 14.8 million millennials, they are forced to work long hours to make ends meet.[2] Further intensifying the need to work, the cost of education (for both advancing millennial parents and their kids) has risen sharply by 65 percent in the last ten years, while the price of food has surged by 26 percent.[3] With inflation and crushing loan repayments going on, our generation is in a significantly worse financial state and well-being than older generations. Whichever the case, neither of these two categories are actually getting the rest that they need.

The longer sleep time may not be a sign of restfulness or concern for physical well-being. As documented in the US National Library for Medicine, excessive sleepiness is a sign of depression, anxiety, boredom, and stress. These are finance-related wellness issues. They are often caused by our inability to earn enough to adequately meet our needs. So, the sleepiness that millennials are experiencing may be attributed to the finance-related stress that a significant number of us face today. But how can we be better? How can we consciously develop better habits that will foster complete wellness?

This chapter breaks down the actions needed to attain complete wellness into five steps. Each step is further broken down into relatable and actionable guides that you can incorporate into your life without disrupting your routine. All of the steps that will be covered in this chapter revolve around you, because wellness is unique to every individual, and you need to find your balance before you can contribute healthily to your surroundings.

STEP #1: BECOME MORE SELF-AWARE

The essence of life varies between people. But it all begins within us. We are who we believe we are. So, our behaviors are in essence a reflection of how we feel inside. Our values, principles, and beliefs. Interestingly, so many people are oblivious to how they feel inside. Worse, some don't know what others think about them. I've realized that a lot of millennials and Gen Zers have seemingly developed a mindset that disregards the opinion of others about them. However, these opinions are like reflections of our actions, which are a reflection of our values and beliefs. Therefore, being self-aware can help you make the best of both how you feel within and how others see you.

Self-awareness is a critical tool for attaining complete wellness. The practice of being self-aware brings you closer to identifying your unique traits. As so many things happen around us simultaneously, we are constantly being torn between ourselves and the environment around us. Being self-aware allows you to get above all the chaos around you to find peace with yourself. It affords you the opportunity to meet yourself as a person, to see yourself from several perspectives.

In simple terms, self-awareness is a state of self-consciousness. It is our ability to monitor what is happening within us, to have a clear eagle-eye view of our inner world. Nevertheless, a lot of people that spend several hours daily reflecting on their lives and actions may not be completely self-aware because there is more to it. To be self-aware requires more than knowing yourself all on your own. It also requires you to see yourself from the lens of others by regularly asking for feedback from the people around you. Therefore, it makes perfect sense when Tasha Eurich, an organizational psychologist, proposes that there are two types of self-awareness.[4]

Types of Self-awareness

1. **Internal self-awareness:** This defines how clearly we see our values, passion, aspirations, environmental fitness, reactions to events, behaviors, strengths, weaknesses, and thoughts. It involves our ability to see how these parts of us affect others around us. This type of self-awareness is particularly important in our everyday lives. It is associated with higher satisfaction in our careers and relationships with others. It also allows us to take control of our personal and social lives. Internal consciousness improves our chances of being happy by reducing the risk of anxiety, stress, and depression.

2. **External self-awareness:** This type of self-awareness is focused on your ability to understand how other people view you. This involves how they see your values, passions, behaviors, strengths, and weaknesses. It's easy to dismiss what others think about us by assuming that they do not know us as much as we know ourselves. While that is true, you stand to gain a lot by understanding their perspective. Some of us may think that we are terrible at certain skills (like leadership or sports), while others think we are exceptionally talented in those areas.

In his book *Perfectly Confident*, Professor Don A. Moore of UC-Berkeley referenced a March 2018 *American Idol* contestant who had the longest and loudest vocal runs. While this singer thought her performance was exceptional and unbeatable, her voice was so loud that it sounded odd and unbearable to hear. Although Katy Perry, a renowned pop singer and one of the judges of the show, brought to her notice the oddness of her voice, the singer dismissed it by saying, "I guess they wanted mediocre singers...I think Katy's just a little jealous she can't hit those notes." She was eliminated from the show right after her performance, and there's no record of her winning any reality show after that one.

Being externally aware will help you to improve upon certain skills, identify and address your social weaknesses, and build sound relationships with those you care about. Unlike the *American Idol* contestant, your chances of growing and winning more at what you do depend on how externally aware you are. It is a good starting point for an occupationally buoyant life. Not only is external awareness tied to career satisfaction, but it is an essential skill for good leadership because it helps you develop empathy for those you are leading. Research shows that the more powerful people get, the less externally self-aware they are and, consequently, their empathy depreciates.

By identifying your behaviors, values, strengths, and weaknesses through internal self-awareness, and knowing how they impact other people, you can build better relationships, accept responsibilities that are more in tune with your personality and values, and have greater control over what pushes your emotions to the extreme. This is one of the abilities that you need to develop.

There are people who are sound in both types of self-awareness, while others could do with a lot more work on both. But the few people who consciously develop both types of awareness are those that you should consider emulating. According to Tasha Eurich, we all are placed in one of four categories of self-awareness.

The Four Self-Awareness Archetypes

This 2x2 maps internal self-awareness (how well you know yourself) against external self-awareness (how well you understand how others see you).

	Low external self-awareness	High external self-awareness
High internal self-awareness	**INTROSPECTORS** They're clear on who they are but don't challenge their own views or search for blind spots by getting feedback from others. This can harm their relationships and limit their success.	**AWARE** They know who they are, what they want to accomplish, and seek out and value others' opinions. This is where leaders begin to fully realize the true benefits of self-awareness.
Low internal self-awareness	**SEEKERS** They don't yet know who they are, what they stand for, or how their teams see them. As a result, they might feel stuck or frustrated with their performance and relationships.	**PLEASERS** They can be so focused on appearing a certain way to others that they could be overlooking what matters to them. Over time, they tend to make choices that aren't in service of their own success and fulfillment.

SOURCE DR. TASHA EURICH

© HBR.ORG

If you fall within the aware category, congratulations! You are among the 15 percent of humans who are completely self-aware. Otherwise you could do with a little more work in that regard. But what should you do exactly?

How to become self-aware

The beauty of self-awareness is that it's not an inborn trait. You can develop this ability and even continuously improve on it. By repeatedly practicing these five steps, you can develop the ability to monitor the world within and around you.

1. **Spend more quiet time with yourself.** When we meet new people, we have to spend some time getting to know them. During those times, we get to understand their values, how they think, their passions, temperaments, and what gets them ticking. As an example that most might be able to identify with, when you're on a date and meeting new people, you might realize that you aren't happy to see them welcome random phone calls that interrupt the conversation and bonding process. The same applies to meeting with yourself.

   Every day, you are taking a new shape. You are learning increasingly better ways of doing things, as well as smarter ways of concluding and deciding on major issues. Without taking the time to check in with yourself regularly, you might miss the lessons that you are gathering. You may not really get to know yourself.

   While a date is good for people you are getting to know, being alone in a quiet place would be a better choice for yourself. You can do it in your bedroom when no one is around, in the corner of your office, in your backyard or a quiet place you'd normally use for mindful meditation or yoga. It could take from a couple of minutes to an hour or more. Perhaps a trip some place where you can appreciate nature by yourself is an even better idea. There you can spend more time bonding with yourself. Whichever option you choose is sure to be a great idea as long as you are not interrupted.

2. **Self-reflect and practice mindfulness regularly.** Many times, our minds replay the events that have happened, the decisions we've made, and our reactions to those incidents. Interestingly, our minds can turn into prediction machines, playing out the possible outcomes of certain actions that we are contemplating. These are wonderful features of our limitless mind. However, they can have a dual effect on our emotional well-being.

Constantly reflecting on your past achievements and victories can be the start of a pompous personality. On the other hand, thinking too much about wrong judgments that you made in the past can hurt your self-confidence. Something similar applies to the predictive function of the brain. When your mind focuses on the possible negative outcomes of a decision, it can lead to anxiety and fear of the unknown. If you spend too much time smiling over the possible positive outcomes of a decision, you may build up expectations that can soon become unrealistic.

Nevertheless, you need this important ability of replaying your past experiences. It makes you aware of the right and wrong decisions that you made, what you could have done better, and how you would approach similar situations in the future. Your ability to project into the future enables you to make proper plans for things that could be coming your way. This can help prepare your mind for rapid changes and overwhelming moments. However, finding a balance between your retrospective and futuristic thinking is crucial. The art of mindfulness can help you do that.

Being mindful keeps you in the present moment at all times. It is the balance between pondering over the past and your concerns about the future. It brings you to the things happening around you. When alone during your quiet times, mindfulness allows you to feel the wind as it graces your skin, the sound of the birds chirping in the woods, the tiny footsteps of your kids as they walk down the hallway, and all other incidents happening at that exact point in time. It allows you to recognize and acknowledge the emotions that you have. However, you are not allowed to act on any of these incidents taking place, except if there's an emergency, of course.

Not acting on your thoughts, feelings, and the things happening around you while you practice mindfulness keeps you in control of your behavior. It keeps you from always reacting. It also stops you from worrying about the unknown yet beautiful future before you.

3. **Ask the "what" questions. Avoid the "why" questions.** When you make the wrong moves, which happens often for some, it's almost a natural response to wonder why it happened that way. "Why" questions always flood our minds when things don't go as

planned. "Why did I not get the promotion?" "Why do I always bomb the SATs every time I give it a try?" "Why can't my business raise any funds for its seed round?"

The "why" questions are endless, and we come up with the right answers for only a few of them. Most of the answers that our brains formulate are designed to doubt our competence or the credibility of what we are doing. This can be distressing and could lead to anxiety and loss of enthusiasm for whatever we are doing. Instead of asking yourself "why" questions during moments of self-reflection, take the time to wonder "what" might have gone wrong.

"What" questions help you point out problems and the direction to follow in order to fix them. They push the brain into the problem-solving zone instead of the critical thinking zone. In the critical thinking zone, you can only identify the problem and wonder if it could be solved. Meanwhile, in the problem-solving zone, our brain identifies obstacles and finds ways to strategically combine sets of available solutions to remove or bypass those obstacles.[5] So, instead of asking those questions mentioned above, ask these: "**What** are the variables that prevented me from getting the promotion, and what can I do to better position myself next time?" "**What** have I been doing wrong in the previous SATs, and **what** do I need to do to ace the next SAT exam?" "**What** do investors need from me and my business to fund this seed round?"

4. **Identify your personality traits.** Don't forget that we are all unique individuals. Our personality defines how we see life and address the challenges that it brings. It is the embodiment of our strengths and weaknesses. Some people are comfortable working on one task at a time, while others excel at multitasking. Some derive pleasure in working alone with little to no supervision or assistance, while others may need someone to always look over their shoulders. During your moments of self-reflection, it's always important to recognize these personality traits.

There are traits that you may not particularly be proud of, but they are yours, and you have to be very honest with yourself about having them. In this way, you can lean into those you are strongest at while you work on developing your weaker traits. There are several personality assessment tests out there for you to confirm what your personality type is. If you quickly search the term "personality test" on Google, you will find links to several assessments. One of my personal favorite assessments is the Insights Discovery Assessment.

5. **Listen to others more and ask for feedback.** The other four steps to follow are focused on helping you develop and improve internal self-awareness. However, external self-awareness can only be gauged by asking for other people's opinions of you in various areas. So, you owe yourself the opportunity to verify your perception of yourself by asking others to share what they think about you.

You may discover that you are not as terrible as you thought you were in some areas while finding out that you could use more work in other areas that you had not considered. Whichever the case, asking others that are close to you and listening attentively to how they believe you could be better will help you identify the new skills to develop as well as the habits to consider dropping. You will connect better with others if they communicate effectively about the behaviors that hurt your feelings. A lot of people tend to keep this displeasure to themselves in their attempt to maintain a relationship. This radical love, as I continue to call it, isn't so healthy for adult relationships. As long as the other person is willing to receive constructive feedback about their behavior, honesty is a core value of the progressive movement. This will help you work on being a better person, building stronger relationships, and maintaining a better state of well-being.

Being self-aware is the first step to knowing yourself. But knowing yourself only brings you closer to achieving wellness. To go any further, you have to be intentional about this journey. You must set goals and devise ways of tracking your goals.

STEP #2: SET WELLNESS GOALS

In the previous section where I discussed the Wellness Wheel, you found out where your wellness journey needs more attention. If yours indicates a need for attention in several areas, you can start off by setting realistic wellness goals that can cover the foundation of your well-being. You could set a financial wellness goal to pay off your debts, starting with the bigger and higher-interest debts. Occupationally, you may consider focusing on a more productive routine or setting a goal that brings you closer to that level in your career that you have always wanted to work toward.

Getting started on this goal-setting journey, the first thing you should do is spend quality personal time connecting with yourself and identifying your personal values, passions, purpose, strengths, and weaknesses. This first step explains how you can make that happen. Thereafter, you can start setting goals that will propel you toward total wellness.

Setting wellness goals is important for several reasons. For one, they are motivating. You are more likely to engage in wellness activities when you have clearly set goals. When you set goals, it's easier for you to ignore distractions and events that will not help you achieve them. However, distractions do exist and could sway you from being on top of your game at all times. But more interestingly, it's easier to identify distractions when you have specific goals and a laid-out plan for achieving them. An easy way to identify distractions, stalling, and procrastination is to weigh whatever you are doing at any moment against your plan and goals. If that activity doesn't bring you closer to accomplishing your goals in any way, then it's a distraction, or you are intentionally keeping yourself from progressing by procrastinating. That's not a very good idea.

Another importance of setting wellness goals is improved mental health. According to a study, clear and specific goal setting improves cognitive retention among millennials and Gen Zers.[6] When we set goals that we genuinely want to pursue to completion, they are buried in our subconscious, and our minds are constantly reminded to follow through on the plans. This constant reminder can help you keep a mental diary of the incidents that are happening around you as you make decisions and take actions that further the accomplishment of your wellness goals.

Professional and personal success is yet another great reason for setting wellness goals. Goals give you a sense of purpose. They give you something to pursue, a sense of adventure that has its rewards. When we check off some tasks that bring us closer to our goals, we are elated and motivated to do more. This takes us up the ladder of accomplishment in our personal lives. Professionally, marking off goals as accomplished can earn you promotions, recognitions, and the respect and admiration of your bosses and colleagues.

The Types of Goals

Depending on your state of well-being, as revealed by the Wellness Wheel exercise, you can define your goals using the 2x2 achievement goal framework developed by A.J. Elliot and H.A. McGregor in 2001.[7] In the framework, they classified goals into four different types. Depending on what direction of your wellness journey you have identified using the Wellness Wheel, place your wellness goal into one of these four categories.

1. **Mastery-approach goals** are set when you are trying to master an activity, a skill, or a habit. When you set mastery-approach goals, you are aiming to be better at what you do by beating records that you've set for yourself. This type of goal is mainly personal, and only you can develop the metrics with which you can measure progress.

2. **Mastery-avoidance goals** are set by some people in certain areas that they don't want to be perceived as ignorant or totally lacking. For instance, you may set a goal to learn how to play chess, not because you really want to become a Grandmaster someday. Rather, you are learning to avoid being a total chess novice. This type of goal isn't really the best option for your wellness journey because you should be concerned about cultivating an unending habit of self-awareness toward becoming a well-rounded person.

3. **Performance-approach goals** are different from mastery. In fact, you may not be concerned about mastering a particular activity. When setting performance-approach goals, your primary focus is to be better than your peers. To run longer distances than your workout buddy. To spend more hours in the yoga studio practicing mindfulness. You may want to be the person that has read the most recent wellness research findings. Whatever the case, the aim of this goal type is not to master an act. It is simply focused on being competitive. This could be a great source of motivation if you have competitive peers that enjoy the excitement of performance-approach goals.

> 4. **Performance-avoidance goals,** on the other hand, may be less intense than the performance approach. This type of goal is not about being the best among your peers. Instead, it is about *not being the worst*. So, your anchor, in this case, can be the lowest-performing person in the group that you are associated with. Your goal is to be better than that person, and maybe a few more people. And it's always cool if you turn out to be the best, but that's not the goal in this case.

Regardless of what type of goal you wish to set for yourself, you have to ensure that it follows a proper framework that will enable you to take the right actions. So, what framework is the best to employ in your goal-setting process?

Using the S.M.A.R.T. Goal framework

In the 1981 issue of *Management Review*, a team of researchers introduced a framework for setting realistic goals.[8] This framework is called the S.M.A.R.T. criteria of goal setting. It requires that your goals be Specific, Measurable, Attainable (in other words, realistic), Relevant (to your purpose and values), and Time-bound (or deadline oriented). Let me explain each of these criteria clearly.

Specific goals are easier for the brain to grasp. Our brain holds on to very simple and clear concepts. It dismisses generic information or treats it as secondary to specific information. So, when setting your wellness goals, be as specific as possible. For instance, your physical wellness goal should be stated somewhat like *"I will walk eight thousand* *steps daily for four days per week.*" And your intellectual wellness goal could be, "*I will read ten pages of a personal finance book every morning.*" The specificity of these goals increases your chance of actually pursuing them because it spells out the place and time for performing these activities.

Measurable goals provide metrics for tracking how well you are doing in your journey toward achieving those goals. Setting an intellectual wellness goal of reading one book every month can be measured weekly if you break the goals down into daily and weekly milestones. If an average book is three hundred pages long, you can consider reading ten pages a day. This will make measuring your progress easier.

Attainability is also crucial for achieving any goal that you set. Unrealistic goals can become discouraging sooner or later. Imagine that you set a spiritual wellness goal of spending half of your waking time praying or connecting with the spiritual part of your being without considering the demands of work, parenting, and other areas of your life. Soon, you may not only drop the goal of spending so much time at your place of prayer, but you will simply abandon the need to visit your prayer place entirely. Making sure to set attainable goals will increase the odds that you will go through with them. Meanwhile, while setting attainable goals, do not forget the element of challenge. Don't set overly challenging goals, but make sure that they are slightly higher than what you have been previously used to. This will stretch your mind, allow you to think bigger, and help you develop a winning mindset.

The **Relevance** of your goal shouldn't be neglected either. Inasmuch as it feels cool to do whatever you want for fun, you just can't always do that. Attaining complete wellness requires intentionality and aligning various tasks with the ultimate goal. So, when setting wellness goals, try your best to ask yourself important questions about their relevance to your core values and life purpose. If they are not relevant in any way, you would be merely procrastinating, moving in the wrong direction, or simply stalling for some reason (perhaps fear).

Time-bound goals are realized faster than timeless wishes. So, when setting your wellness goals, make sure to set a timeline for achieving those goals. This introduces a sense of urgency into the equation and helps you think outside the box to get it done faster or in time, at the very least. An example of a time-bound (or SMART) goal may be:

> *"I will have an emergency fund of $50,000 in a personal safe box by* **December 14, 2025**, *which I will build by making monthly $1,300 deposits into said box."*

The monthly goal of saving $1,300 is considered relevant to the bigger goal of having a $50,000 emergency fund by 2025. This bigger goal is, in turn, relevant to your financial well-being.

STEP #3: IDENTIFY YOUR STRENGTHS, LIMITATIONS, AND STRESSORS

Everyone has something they are good at. We also have something we are not good at. That's acceptable. It is what makes each of us unique. However, how we approach this uniqueness determines whether we will be happy or struggle through life from time to time. So, it is important for you to identify the things that you are genuinely good at. They are called your strengths, and focusing on them can help you live a happier life. But how can you find your strengths?

Strengths are products of talents. Your talents are your natural pattern of thinking. They are the feelings and behaviors that give you the potential to do something really well.[9] And as you already know, everybody has a natural thought pattern. Some have similar thought patterns, while others have entirely different thought patterns. These different people are sometimes considered weird or outliers. They are seldom classified as average humans. However, some people have become exceptional at what they do by investing a lot of time and effort into developing their talents. A fully developed talent is what is referred to as a strength (or competence). So, if everyone has talents that could be developed into strengths, how can you identify yours?

Identify your strengths

Spending quality quiet time alone, reflecting on your life and the activities that you've engaged in, is a proven way of identifying your strengths. Since we all have at least one talent that could grow into a strength, we have at some point used it with (or without) really knowing that we were using an inborn talent. Therefore, while reflecting, you should consider the following clues to help you identify what you are naturally good at.

1. **Fervor:** While you reflect on your previous engagements, identify the activities that made you glad you got involved. This type of engagement makes you want to have more experience. Did you join a nonprofit organization exploring the chances of eradicating malaria in West Africa some years ago, or did you assist the product team in finding and fixing a bug in one of your tech products? Did you really enjoy it and wish for it to happen again? If you did, then you must have some passion for such activity, and it could possibly be one of your strengths. Take note.

2. **Quick learning:** This is another factor to consider when looking out for your strengths. If strengths are products of talents (a natural thought pattern), then it shouldn't be so hard to pick up the required skills to perform the activities that require your strengths. You just find yourself doing them with less difficulty than someone whose thought pattern is entirely different. Therefore, while reflecting, quickly note the activities that make you feel like a natural.

3. **Flow:** When you are naturally good at something without the need to put much effort in, it's very unlikely that you need dedicated, by-the-minute supervision to get it done. You instinctively know what to do next. Because your thought pattern aligns with the activity, your instinct tells you what to do next at each stage. You may need to ask questions a

few times to reaffirm that you are on track, but you are right on track most of the time. Keep a record of the activities that bring flow out of you effortlessly.

4. **Satisfaction:** When you have a fervor for a particular activity that brings out the best in you, there is a great chance that it will come out great or better than you thought. When this happens, you feel a sense of satisfaction from the work that you've done, whether or not it was perfect. Keep an eye out for such activities. It's a good place to start exploring your strengths.

On the flip side, our weaknesses are those activities that make us uncomfortable. They cause great distress, and we find ourselves swearing deep down every time we are required to perform them. Nevertheless, you have to accept the fact that sometimes, you will be required to perform tasks and engage in activities that you don't particularly enjoy. This is less of a problem since you only have to do it once in a blue moon.

Learn your limitations

By focusing on your strengths and developing them further, you can find happiness and satisfaction in the things you do. You will be more productive and more engaged in your work, with your fitness, meditation, environment, and life in general. However, knowing your strengths may not be the only thing required to harness them effectively. **You also have to be aware of your limitations**.

Even though you choose to ignore your weaknesses and focus on your strengths, limitations exist to make certain conditions unfavorable for you. Depending on your personality, environment, and health conditions, limitations vary. Some are within your control, while others are not.

Uncontrollable limitations may include disabilities, incurable disorders, and deficiencies (like ADHD). Regardless of how much you enjoyed driving and how effortlessly you did it on the first try, you may not be well suited to a career in Formula One driving if you have a severe eye defect, anxiety disorder, or PTSD. This is because it increases the risk of fatal incidents occurring. And even though you are very good at driving, it's just not worth the undue risk.

Controllable limitations, on the other hand, are within your grasp. You have the power to stop these limitations from jeopardizing your pursuit of wellness. Excessive drinking, smoking, excessive caffeine consumption, and other addictions are examples of controllable limitations. People could also be a limitation to your pursuit of wellness. Sometimes we encounter people around us that make us feel less competent, demeaned, or unworthy. You may have to review your relationship with them and either cut them off entirely or significantly reduce your association with them. I'm referring to both the people and the substances that are directly limiting your potential.

Achieving total wellness can become increasingly difficult if your uncontrollable limitations are aggravated by toxic habits that place controllable limitations in your way. For someone that is attention deficient and hypersensitive, high caffeine consumption may not be a good idea. Although studies have shown that caffeine, as a stimulant, mimics certain ADHD medications, its independent and excessive use may aggravate the hypersensitive part of anybody with the condition.[10] By practicing self-awareness, reflecting on how you feel under certain conditions, and taking note of these, you will find a way to overcome these limitations.

Handle stressors

There are everyday events that may pose a challenge to your well-being. These are not caused by your actions, genetic composition, or even personality. They are not unique to anyone, although we react to them somewhat differently. They are called **stressors** and exist in varying intensities. Stressors are a constant that exists in every area of one's wellness journey, actively causing emotional distress. Financial strains, troubling family interactions, heavy New York traffic, hiatuses at work, and constant admonitions from a boss (just to name a few) are examples of everyday stressors. And as I mentioned earlier in previous chapters, stress is a major cause of anxiety and depression in our world today. Finding a way to effectively manage it can make all the difference you need.

Depending on the intensity of the stress caused by these stressors, its effect and method of management vary. **High-level stress** is troubling to everyone involved and leaves cautionary signals that many people address almost immediately. Is a job draining you mentally or a friend abusing you physically? These are easy to identify as stressors and should be avoided immediately.

Low-grade stressors, on the other hand, aren't as easily identifiable. Low-grade stressors, like commuting through multiple routes to drop off the kids at school and then to work every day may cause minimal stress that may not be a cause for alarm. Constantly experiencing this type of stress, however, can have chronic effects on your emotional and physical well-being over time.[11] As a matter of fact, the World Health Organization reports that stress is one of the leading causes of premature death in developed nations. And while high-level stressors can be identified from a distance, it's often difficult to put a pin on low-grade stressors. Sometimes it's nearly impossible to see them as causative agents.

Despite stress levels, one very potent way to manage stress is through exposure to nature. Frequently visiting green places can significantly lower stress and enhance the restorative effect of the plants around us.[12] A study in Japan (*Shinrin-yoku*) shows that forest bathing (frequently walking in the forest to observe and absorb nature) helps to improve immune response and reduce the risk of depression.[13] So, nature's greenness is a known antidote to stress of all levels.

Witnessing the decline of the planet's greenery within the last half decade due to global warming and wildfires, it has been quite troubling to imagine the effect it could have on us. It is up to us to be environmentally responsible by planting and nurturing trees and other green lives, reducing energy consumption, saving water, and using eco-friendly products. These environmentally friendly activities are in line with our well-being since they make nature available for our therapeutic needs.

STEP #4: DEVELOP CRITICAL SKILLS

A major cause of unwellness is stress. It either comes from the activities that we engage in or the people we interact with. Sometimes it's physical. At other times it's emotional, financial, or spiritual. Whichever it is, you need to hone the skills required to help you get through it consistently. Some of the essential skills that you need to develop include emotional awareness and intelligence, time management, and coping skills.

Be emotionally aware

Emotional awareness is critical because it allows you to interact with your feelings. Being emotionally aware means that you can recognize and express how you feel at any particular time, as well as identify its cause. Without knowing exactly what or how you are feeling and its underlying cause, it is difficult to control or change your emotional state. Being aware of your feelings will positively influence your social well-being by helping you develop stronger relationships with people through effective communication of emotions. With the ability to identify, interpret, and control your emotions comes an elevated level of self-esteem. You earn the admiration of others for your ability to effectively articulate/communicate your emotional state. You can develop an awareness for your feelings by paying close attention to the incidents that caused a particular emotion and recognizing the effect of that emotion on you.

These steps may help you become better aware of your emotions.

1. **Evaluate causative incidents:** Things don't just happen. Our feelings are reactions to something that happened or that is happening around us. Is it the memory of a loved one that makes you feel sad? The thought of home that makes you feel nostalgic? Whatever it is that's making you feel some way, take the time to evaluate it. Try to figure out why it happened and why it made you feel the way you did. Was it the expectations that you built, the plans that you had, or efforts that seemed wasted?

2. **Pinpoint your bodily reactions:** When incidents happen, our body reacts in some uncontrollable way. It's the brain's way of creating an experience. Depending on how an incident makes you feel, your skin might pale, muscles tighten, heartbeat change, or cold shivers travel throughout your body in an instant. Whichever it is, you will know whether it was pleasant or terrifying.

After these signals sent by the brain travel through our body, we often spring into voluntary action. You may find yourself smiling or frowning; withdrawing, freezing to the spot, or moving toward things or people; or experience some changes in the pitch and tone of your voice. All these may happen so fast that you might miss them. But when you sit back to reflect on them, you will realize that despite being fast, they can be isolated, explained, and improved upon.

3. **Determine the intensity of the emotion felt**: We all feel the same emotion in different ways. For some people, intense joy can cause them to break into tears, while others cry when they are angry. How you respond to emotions is unique to you. So, by knowing that uniqueness, during your moments of reflection, you can determine the intensity of the emotions that you felt. Was it too much for you? Did you feel overwhelmed? Did it ruin your whole day? How exactly did you handle it?

4. **Keep an emotion journal**: Keeping all these observations in your head may cloud your mind and make your reflection really slow. So, instead of sorting them all out in your head, write about them. Describe them in your journal. This will clear your thoughts and allow you to see things more clearly. Also, a journal is preferable to a random piece of paper. Journals offer a way for you to look

> back at the notes that you've taken. They allow you to build upon previous observations and track changes in your behavior and improvement in your ability to be aware of (and control) your emotions.

Build emotional intelligence

Emotional awareness is only one piece of the pie. The bigger pie when it comes to control over emotions is **emotional intelligence** (simply referred to as EQ). It encompasses your ability to identify and manage your emotions as well as recognize and influence the emotions of those around you.[14] And because our actions are inspired by how we feel, great leaders use EQ to get everyone on their team aligned with the organization's mission and values. But you don't have to be a corporate executive to see the need to improve your EQ.

EQ accounts for almost 90 percent of what differentiates successful and fulfilled people from less happy people.[15] Being smart, or a genius, can help you get work done on your own. However, work in today's world is overwhelming. There's so much to do, and you can't seem to do it all alone. You need the help of other people at various points in time. EQ is the magical tool that helps you to connect with these people and influence how they feel. It is your ticket to establishing very healthy relationships with the people around you. It brings out the empathy in you, allowing you to imagine yourself in the situation of others, understanding how they might be feeling, and offering effective ways to help or avoid aggravating situations for them.

Furthermore, people with high EQ earn the respect of others easily because they treat people with respect both for their personality and their feelings. As a result, it has a high impact on job satisfaction. According to psychologist Daniel Goleman, EQ is the most important quality that people should have because it trumps expertise and technical skills in shared spaces. People with high EQ have developed ways of remaining calm under immense pressure and are good at resolving conflicts with colleagues, friends, and family members. Interestingly, everyone can improve their EQ. So, if emotional awareness is only one part of EQ, how do you develop the other areas?

If you have taken the time to become aware of your emotions, you have successfully completed the first phase of becoming emotionally intelligent. These next steps will help you understand and influence the emotions of those around you.

1. **Ask the right questions and listen actively:** Sometimes people need someone to speak to, and other times, they need someone to listen. Just walking up to a random person may not be ideal, so you might consider practicing this with someone you're close to, possibly a colleague, friend, or family member. They need to be asked what the problem is. You will often get the "I'm all right" response when you ask people how they are doing. Their responses are often laced with emotional clues that tell you that they are not really all right but are only being courteous. I know you may be dealing with a lot of your own issues too. You don't necessarily have to help others solve their

problems if, for whatever reason, it'll create additional undue pressure or hardship for you, but a listening ear could be the ultimate help that a person needs to avoid looming episodes of depression.

2. **Stay motivated:** It's difficult for you to recognize and care about the feelings of others if you are dragging yourself all over the place. Being aware of your own emotional state, you may recognize events that could dampen your mood. So, avoid them. This can help you stay on top of your moods, making it easier for others to feel the same way. Remember that feelings are contagious. Nevertheless, it's not realistic for you to think that you will be motivated every day. There are bad days and good days alike. Simply doing your best to recognize what makes a good day turn bad helps you to avoid them as often as you can.

3. **Give and receive constructive feedback:** When you deal with people around you, there will be differences to resolve and broken expectations to mend. When someone acts in a manner that doesn't sit well with you, do your best not to talk to them harshly about it. Instead, constructively express your displeasure in a tone that won't hurt their feelings, but offer suggestions on how they can improve. The first step to giving constructive feedback is building trust and restraining yourself from judging the person before you hear from them. It is not advisable to dismiss them as not good or assume the intention for their actions. Walk up to them and try as much as you

can to give them the feedback face to face. Be honest about what you think they might be doing wrong, but don't forget to acknowledge the things that they have done right, no matter how little. It's very possible for you to dabble in other areas of the project and even veer into personal conversations, but you should not do that. Stay focused on the issues that you are addressing, and be as respectful as you can be about it. While you're giving feedback, however, don't forget that you are not all-knowing. You may wrong others too. Be open to criticism, consider suggestions, and make the commitment to improve yourself.

Manage time effectively

Effective time management is another critical skill that you must develop to help you attain full wellness. Regardless of your level of self-awareness and emotional intelligence, the major obstacle to complete wellness is stress. Nobody exhibits stress more than someone who is managing their time poorly.

1. **Prioritize.** To be able to manage your time effectively, you need to learn to prioritize your engagements. There are only twenty-four hours in one day, and there's a limit to what you can do within those hours. So, you should make a list of everything you have on your plate and organize it in order of priority. Complete the items that are most impactful, and that will give you the highest sense of satisfaction

when you complete them. Without doing this, you may find yourself getting overwhelmingly busy with everything and nothing. Working around the clock and getting nothing done can make anyone go insane. Guard your emotional well-being and prioritize.

2. **Delegate.** You can't do it all on your own. Ask people who are skilled in specific tasks to handle them for you. You may be better at the task than they are, but you have to trust them well enough to get it done at least 80 percent as well as you would. This will help you free up time to focus on the activities right on top of your priority list. This way, you will do a lot more by the end of the day than you might have managed on your own.

3. **Block out time.** If you don't put everything in its place on your calendar, your day might feel scattered and disorganized. Ensure to block out times for certain activities, including exercise, meditation, lunch, emails, etc. According to Kevin Kruse in his book *15 Secrets Successful People Know About Time Management,* you should make sure to block out time for everything and ignore whatever didn't make it into your calendar, except for serious emergencies.

Identify your coping skills

It doesn't matter how religious you are with the guides to wellness out there; life happens, and oftentimes we are thrown off balance. Sometimes we can't change anything, and we have to live through it. Occupationally, there are times when the responsibilities on us feel crushing. Intellectually, there are times when we hit a wall and struggle with learning. How do you remain on track? How do you keep your head high, maintain optimum emotional well-being, and stay resilient?

To be able to do these things, you need coping skills that help you look past the thick smoke of challenges and stressful events. These skills help you stay on track with a laid-out plan to achieve your personal and professional goals. You should note, though, that coping skills are unique to situations and individuals. I will briefly discuss the common coping skills that work for many people. Perhaps you can find a way to make them work for you.

1. **Feel hopeful:** The feeling of hope is one of the strongest emotions that boosts your positivity. I refer to hope as a harmless form of expectation that may be met but never stings us when it's not. It's a drive that makes us want to keep going in hard times. It is the belief that if only we keep on doing our best and move in the right direction, there will be a reward for our efforts. Interestingly enough, there is a reward most of the time. So, if you stay hopeful, you are more likely to overcome the temporary challenges that you may be facing at a new job, with your complex family, or in the new routine that you have adopted in a bid to improve your wellness.

2. **Exercise regularly:** When some people are over-whelmed, they take a walk or run, use the gym, or

engage in some form of aerobic exercise. Some people visit the golf course, soccer field, or basketball pitch. And these activities have been shown to be very helpful in dealing with stress. The science behind it is quite simple. When we engage in aerobic exercise, our body releases feel-good chemicals (like adrenaline, cortisol, and endorphin) into the blood that make us feel relieved, relaxed, and ready to face the challenges that are before us. For many people, exercising is an excellent coping mechanism. It could work for you too.

3. **Acknowledge and healthily express your feelings:** Whenever we feel strongly about someone's actions, it hurts us more to bottle it up. So, instead of bottling it up for whatever reason, you will be in a better place emotionally when you acknowledge that you have strong feelings and respectfully express your feelings to the people around you or the person that inspired such feelings. For instance, if your partner makes a hurtful comment, you should recognize and accept the fact that you were hurt by the comment. Thereafter, you can express your displeasure to them at the right time and in a way that will be least likely to put them on the defensive.

4. **Unplug from the media:** Information overload is another cause of distress, especially during the pandemic. People get emotionally drained by following the news and social media posts from influencers and their old friends. Although social networking platforms are a part of our everyday lives today, it will

always help you to unplug from them regularly. You don't need to be on top of every story that's happening around the world. You also don't have to get worked up over events that you can't do anything to change. These are emotionally draining, especially for people with an empathic personality type (empaths). Empaths are always imagining themselves in positions that other people are in and trying to empathize even with fictional characters. This can be distressing. Overuse of social media platforms can expose empaths to an overload of incidents that send them on a downward emotional spiral. So, discipline yourself to unplug from the internet regularly.

7 Reliable Coping Strategies to Try

1. Make time to exercise and unwind every day.

2. Accept yourself and your limitations.

3. Associate with people that accept you too.

4. Set realistic deadlines for projects.

5. Break down your tasks into smaller steps.

6. Jot down ideas as they come to you.

7. Handle one task at a time, beginning with the most important ones.

STEP #5: ALWAYS EXECUTE WITH DISCIPLINE

Now that you have an idea of what it means to be self-aware, I'm fairly confident that you will try to improve upon your self-awareness. I'm sure you have some wellness goals that have been sitting in the back of your mind for quite some time. Have you always wanted to look physically fit, to switch to a vegan diet, to go out more, drink less, read more, reflect more, or even travel more? I'll bet you have one or more of these on your list of goals.

How about the things you can (or cannot) do? Have you come to peace with your inabilities (or areas of growth) and embraced your strengths? How about your limitations? Do you recognize them now? Have you decided on what to do to break through to achieve total wellness?

The important skills that will help you build stronger relationships, do more work that you love, and live the life that you've always wanted are also at your disposal. Perhaps you recognize the ones you already have in your arsenal and can now identify those you need to develop. Whichever the case, nothing can happen until you take the necessary steps to make things happen. Complete soundness of body and mind won't creep up on you by coincidence. You have to take the actions required to make you emotionally, physically, intellectually, financially, and spiritually fit. And inasmuch as everyone wants to take those actions, only a few people do. Why is that?

To be disciplined requires you to say no to a lot of things that may be enticing. Discipline requires people to do the right things at the right time, even when we don't feel like doing it. To discipline yourself to stay on a healthy meal plan will require you to decline an offer of free pizza and ignore cravings that will not help your nutritional goals come true. Everyone has the ability to do this, but not a lot of people have the will strong enough to resist their deepest desires. To attain total wellness, you have to try your best. You are not perfect. No one is. You may slide off track at some point, but you must want to achieve these wellness goals deeply enough that you find your way back on track. To be able to achieve this, you need to execute your goals with intense discipline.

Disciplined execution isn't just about taking action. Rather, it is about having a plan, sticking to it, and executing each step without ceasing. It is about focusing on your goals and consistently taking the required actions needed to meet them.

Maintaining this level of discipline consistently isn't easy, but it is achievable. Merely leaving the chances of you making things happen to your free will alone may be very demanding. This high demand makes it easier for anyone to give up and settle for just living through life, one day at a time. While this isn't a very bad idea, losing hope and focus on your wellness goals can triple the risk of depression. Therefore, to make it easier for you to execute your wellness plans with discipline, keep these four important questions in your mind at all times and continue seeking answers to them.

What is most important right now?

In shared spaces, homes, and social events, almost everything seems to be important. But not all of them are.

At least not to you. When you are swamped with a lot of options (as we often are), it's fairly easy to jump on the next available option or the easiest one. You may want to talk to the next sociable person at an event, but is that the person you should be holding a conversation with right now?

You could have a lot of tasks to complete at the organization that you work for, so you decide to start working on the next or easiest task right away. Did you take some time to ponder if that's the most important task at that moment?

Some people just live life as it comes to them. While that is a pretty fair idea, it may not be best for your well-being. So, make the commitment to always ask yourself this question, "What is most important right now?" before engaging in any new activity. Giving yourself an honest answer will immensely help you get through tons of distractions on your wellness journey. It saves you great time and energy.

What leverage do I have?

This question is just as important as the first. You may choose to engage in the right activity, one that will create the greatest impact on your well-being, but lack the skills or strengths to perform it. This could cause more frustration than satisfaction during the process.

For instance, if you do not have the actual skills required to complete a task for your boss, you may have the ability to influence someone else who is exceptionally skilled in that area to help you out. In this case, your influence on a skilled colleague is your leverage.

So, identifying your leverage before you execute your plans will make it easier for you to stay disciplined. Remember that when the road gets tough, those with leverage keep going.

How do I know if I'm succeeding?

After defining your wellness goals, it is important for you to create checklists of the things that you need to be doing to achieve those goals, as well as outline the results that are expected when the items on your checklist are completed. You can create daily checklists that outline what you should be doing for yourself and others each day. The activities on these checklists must be relevant to your goal. So, they have to bring you closer to attaining total wellness each time.

Creating the right checklist matters a lot. And tracking the right results matter even more. For some wellness activities, creating a checklist and tracking results is relatively straightforward. A weight loss goal, for instance, inspires a checklist that includes working out, eating a low-fat and low-carb diet, and using the scale to check your weight. Tracking the results is also straightforward: how much weight (in pounds or kilograms) was shed in the last week?

For other wellness activities like meditation and forest bathing, it's hard to track the results in real time, even though incorporating them into your daily routine may be fairly easy. Not seeing real-time results for an activity that is taking up considerable amounts of time in your day can be demotivating. Therefore, it is crucial for you to figure out how you can determine whether or not you are succeeding in your pursuit of complete wellness.

In the case of meditation and forest bathing, journaling can be of great help. Use a reflection journal to keep track of how you respond to situations around you, especially frequently recurring and typically distressing events. You will realize over time that your responses may become less defensive, and you are less anxious about those events. You will also begin to take notice of smaller, less significant details that used to slip through your observations unnoticed once you consistently journal your reflections.

How do I hold myself accountable?

This is the trickiest question to answer. Some people tend to dismiss this question in the belief that they can always hold themselves accountable in some way. Others believe that they will figure it out as they go, which is not necessarily a bad idea. But the risk of relapsing and letting a lack of discipline creep up on you becomes greater if you don't have an accountability system in place.

Usually, an accountability partner is invaluable in this case. An accountability partner is someone with whom you review your progress and challenges on a regular basis (weekly, monthly, or quarterly, as the case may be). With an accountability partner, you are more likely to execute your plans with discipline because it gives you this inborn urge to want to prove to them that you can keep to the plan.

However, finding a good partner to help you stay on track can be quite challenging, especially when you are trying to change your circle or pursuing a goal that the people around you don't really believe in. Keeping yourself accountable by gamifying (e.g., applying typical elements of game playing to an activity, such as point scoring, competition with others, and rules of play) your progress can be helpful. Referring back to the weight loss example above, you can print and hang a calendar on your wall to record your weight measurement daily. This will give you the urge to want to keep track of your weight and actively work toward achieving the goals that you've set for yourself.

Bonus: How To Develop Self-Discipline

To achieve total wellness, we need to be disciplined. It helps us create a plan and stick to it and take action even when we don't feel like it. Discipline is what you need to wake up early in the morning to start your day or to pick up a book and read it to the end. It is needed to quit smoking and stop excessive drinking. It is considered the ultimate recipe for success. Interestingly, no one is born with a high level of discipline. It is an acquired trait, and you too can develop it. With the following steps, you can begin your journey toward self-discipline.

1. **Acknowledge the challenges that might keep you from reaching a particular goal.** As was mentioned earlier, we are each unique in our own ways. While one person may consider nighttime as the most productive hours, another person may find it difficult to keep their eyes open when it's nighttime. You know yourself better than anyone else. So, you know what works for you and what doesn't. If you are not sure what your challenges really are, you should consider spending more time with yourself, practicing the art of mindfulness.

   Recognizing the challenges that you face is one thing; acknowledging and accepting them is another. There are some challenges that we can change with ease, while there are others that will require a lot of energy to overcome. Others may be unchangeable. Identify each of them, and accept that there's nothing you can do to change the unchangeable ones. This way, you can make plans to thrive despite those challenges. It will be more difficult to stay disciplined if you have to struggle with challenges often.

2. **Create a clear plan for reaching your goal.** Some people believe that they can plan as they progress. However, many of the people that believe this seldom reach their goals. So, instead of dismissing the need to plan, take your time to plan all the way through to the end. It's okay for things to change along the way.

As long as you remain flexible, you can overcome any challenges that emerge as you progress, and you will always find your way back to the plan. When making plans, make sure they are realistic. Unrealistic plans can demoralize you along the way and cause you to give up on your goals.

3. **Remove temptations and distractions.** When creating your plan, it is important to identify the things that you know could potentially stop, delay, or cause you to look the other way from achieving your goal. It could be the packs of cigarettes or an ashtray that's always around the house or the bottles of soda in the refrigerator. It could be your smartphone that's always on your desk whenever you are trying to read a book or the TV when it's time to go to bed. Whatever the temptation or distraction, as long as it reminds you of something you shouldn't be doing, you should remove it from your immediate environment.

Replace these distractions and temptations with something that reminds you to take the appropriate actions. You should consider replacing the sodas in the fridge with bottles of water. Take away the ashtray and keep a bowl of fruit on the dining table instead. Keep the phone in the living room or far away from you when you want to read and keep a book close to your bed so you can be reminded to read before bedtime. This is referred to as **environmental redesigning,** and it can help you stay disciplined.

4. **Visualize the reward and trust the process.** Most times, what keeps disciplined people going is the vision that they have ingrained in their thoughts. The vision of winning an Olympic gold medal inspires Olympians to commit to training every day, to continuously improve themselves. The thought of being intellectually buoyant can inspire you to continue pursuing your goal. When you keep your eye on the reward, you will be less likely to find quick hacks to accomplish your goals. You will commit to the process, and you will see it through because you have a clear vision of how you want things to look in the end. Until that happens, you are very likely to stay undisciplined.

5. **Reassess yourself whenever you slip off track.** Nobody is 100 percent disciplined. At least, not on the first try. Even the most disciplined people you see today have made mistakes, cheated, or have at times accidentally stopped taking the right actions. However, they were able to reassess themselves and rediscover the reason why they had committed toward achieving their goals in the first place. Reassessing yourself will help you identify your mistakes, what you've done wrong, and how you slipped off track. Then you can create a better plan to avoid those distractions and temptations that led to the mistakes in the first place. Now, you can give it another attempt. You should keep in mind, though, that you may slip off track more than once. Your ability to reassess yourself and your actions every time you go off plan, cheat, or make mistakes will always draw your attention back to the actual plan, reward, and process.

Key Takeaways

1. Being self-aware helps you to identify your passions, strengths, challenges, and to further define your values (internal self-awareness). It also makes you aware of how other people see you so that you can act accordingly (external self-awareness).

2. Focus on the "whats" and worry less about the "whys."

3. You can set goals to either be the best at a particular thing or to avoid being the worst at that thing.

4. To make your goals easier to accomplish, you should set them using the S.M.A.R.T. goals framework (Simple, Measurable, Attainable, Relevant, and Time-bound).

5. Regularly unwind by spending time observing and appreciating nature. This is an effective way of managing stress and recovering fast from negative emotions.

PART THREE

Extending the Goodness

CHAPTER SIX

Parental Wellness

More than half of the world's children today are parented by millennials, the generation born between 1977 and 1995. In the United States, twenty-two million millennials are parents already.[1] That's over 30.5 percent of all millennials in America. And to put things into more context, the number of millennial parents continues to grow, as approximately nine thousand children are born every day. However, it's not a mystery that the millennial parenting style is vastly different from that of their parents. Millennials practice more of a positive parenting style, giving their kids quality time and instilling a positive mindset into them rather than exercising authority as was the style of parenting for most parents of previous generations.

Many millennials had a vastly different upbringing and world experience from their parents of older generations. They experienced several economic and financial downturns, as well as an opioid crisis that started in the 1990s and affected over 10.1 million young millennials, among which more than seventy thousand lost their lives in 2019.[2] But they are significantly more educated and positive than older generations. For this reason, they are nurturing their kids in ways that they believe are better. They are showing affection and are actively planning for the future of their children. Sixty-six percent of millennials today are already saving up for their children's college education. That's almost twice the efforts of baby boomers (35 percent).[3] If most millennials have a free-hand parenting style and, as such, are less stern toward their children, should we consider it a good thing? Are there better ways to raise children? Could we even do better?

While I may not be an expert in parenting or a childhood psychology consultant, it is very important to observe that these kids are growing up in a world that is advancing at an overwhelming pace. The rapid changes happening around them can cause cognitive dissonance. This is because they will be constantly forced to adapt to new environmental and social conditions, even before the changes happen. Interestingly, we cannot stop these changes from happening, but we can raise our kids to keep cool heads while they navigate them. And this is not an easy feat because there is so much more to handle than just raising kids alone.

In 2020, alongside having kids, almost 50 percent of millennials were already taking care of their aging parents.[4] This requires a lot of time and financial investment. Considering the fact that an average millennial has a net worth averaging just slightly more than $8,000, these responsibilities can result in significant financial strains, sinking them deeper into debt on top of student loans and credit card entanglements.[5] But who would they leave their aging parents for?

That is why they are referred to as the sandwich generation.[6] The unique responsibilities that millennials manage can lead to a serious lapse in wellness for those who aren't so skilled at multitasking. It turns out, though, that millennials are not alone. Some of the oldest Gen Zers are graduating college, getting married, and having kids. Although their parents are relatively young and the need for their care may not be so closely imminent, they face almost the same challenges that the preceding generation, millennials, are dealing with.

This chapter explains why you need to treat the wellness of your kids as a priority, what your wellness responsibilities to your kids are, and how you can help them build a solid foundation for a sustainably better well-being without losing focus of your own. While the objective of this chapter is not to teach you how to be a better parent, it offers noteworthy suggestions that could help parents avoid raising distressed kids.

WELLNESS AND PARENTING OVERLAP

Previous generations may dismiss the emotional risks that kids face, and because of that incorrect assumption, conclude that kids know so little and have so little to worry about that could lead to anxiety or even fear. Today, it's difficult to dismiss the fact that kids face the same wellness risk that adults do. In 2020, the New York Times reported that 2–3 percent of children between the ages of six and seventeen suffer from depression.[7] Also, a whopping 7 percent of kids have anxiety disorders that could develop into depression. What's interesting is that these kids have a hard time expressing themselves. So, it is your responsibility as a parent to know when your kid is repeatedly having mood battles and help seek professional help. This responsibility is more challenging during the pandemic than it was before. Now, parents are keeping their kids safe from unprotected social gatherings, preventing them from socializing as they used to with the intention of keeping them safe. They are also being careful to make sure that these kids are not completely stripped of their ability to socialize. As a way to help, many parents are helping their kids engage with communities virtually, using e-learning platforms, and spending more family time together, playing familiar games. Even with all these times together, how do you know that your kid could be struggling?

> It's hard to tell when a child is struggling with depression, but observant parents are more likely to notice the signs early.

Anxiety and depression are relatively new to children. They may have a hard time expressing their feelings and sharing how they are feeling because they may not have the words to describe it. Moreover, not a lot of adults can clearly explain their feelings of anxiety and depression. One of the best ways to help familiarize kids with these weird feelings is to discuss them. Making mental health discussions a part of everyday life is essential to helping your kids understand that they can be understood and helped with whatever issue they are feeling.[8] Nevertheless, you may have to ask them some questions when you notice behavioral changes.

While you ask your children questions about their well-being, don't just listen to what they have to say. Do more by paying close attention to their behavioral changes. Dr. Maria Kovacs, professor of psychiatry at the University of Pittsburgh School of Medicine, advises that parents and guardians pay attention to the things that children begin to do or stop doing. She describes the down feeling that you may observe in your kids as irritability, although many parents tend to dismiss it as sadness.

When children are feeling anxious or fearful, which is common among very young children, they tend to lash out or withdraw. If this anxiety lingers, their feelings begin to drop chronically. They may find that making friends and talking to people is not so helpful because they believe that no one can understand or help them. Just as adults struggle to get out of this unpleasant mood, children have to struggle even harder. And without the ability to pinpoint the issue, helplessness and frustration set in. This may be expressed by your child as lingering anger or crankiness. It is equally common among kids that have ADHD.[9]

Sometimes children suffering from depression lose energy and tire quickly. They become disinterested in engaging in social activities and develop unusual sleeping patterns. Some begin to sleep more, while others start losing sleep. Loss of appetite is also common among children that are struggling with things they can't seem to describe. Physical symptoms like body aches, headaches, and stomach upset are also common complaints that kids give to parents when they are going through one of these bouts of overwhelming negative emotions. And the worst part is that they are often concerned about something more than what they are feeling.

Possible Signs of Depression to Look out for in Kids

- Increased or decreased appetite
- Low energy/enthusiasm
- Hard-to-explain feelings of hopelessness
- Guilt
- Loss of concentration/interest in regular activities
- High sensitivity to rejection
- Regular and unusual anger and outbursts from minor irritations
- Social withdrawal

More than you know, children are aware of how their actions affect those around them. Snapping at things and people sends them further downward in that spiral. Eventually, they completely disengage from activities around the house and in school. This is a terrible place for anyone to be, let alone kids. To express how horrifying it can be, 41 percent of hospital emergency visits between 2007 and 2015 were kids below eleven years old with suicidal thoughts. As of 2018, suicide was the second leading cause of death among children aged ten to fourteen years. Why is this happening to kids, and what can you do to help yours?

1. **Observations are not enough. Ask the right questions.** Making thorough observations is crucial, but there are other reasons why a child may lose interest in activities, appetite, or sleep. They may be signs of other conditions that could be addressed early enough to avoid complications. For instance, a child with learning disabilities or ADHD may feel frustrated with school activities, especially in the early stages when you (the parent) are yet to discover the issue. While kids may not be able to identify what they are feeling, asking the right questions can help you uncover what the root of the actual problems may be.

   While asking these questions, however, you have to be careful. Remember that they are kids, and seemingly harmless ideas can metamorphose in their mind into something harmful. If you are worried that your child may be depressed and having suicidal thoughts, ask them outright if they have such thoughts. So, be very sensitive with the type of questions that you ask children, as well as how you ask them.

2. **Identify stressors and address them.** When kids drift into depressing moods, they are usually thrown into them by distressing events. It could be a quick change in environment, school, neighborhood of residence, or playgroup. Research has found that frequent moves can significantly affect a child's social-emotional well-being.[10] However, the same

study revealed that the effect of this change varies depending on the age of the child. Most of the time, relocating requires your child to change schools and meet new people. This can have an immediate effect on the child's intellectual well-being that, if not addressed, can linger into their adult life.

Loss of a loved one (expected or not) and parents' divorce are also leading causes of childhood depression. Kids are really attached to their friends, siblings, parents, and even familiar neighbors. When situations occur and those friends or neighbors have to move away, the child is affected psychologically. In the case of death, children face a huge risk of emotional unwellness and imminent depression.[11] However, depending on who is deceased, a strong support system could be really helpful. In the event that parents are affected by the same loss, children seldom get the strong support to help them get through that downward spiral.

There are social stressors that could lead to prolonged anxiety. Bullying in school, for example, can leave severe scars in the minds of children, causing anxiety and disengagement from academic activities and heightened risks of depression. About 20 percent of children report being bullied in school, and only a small proportion of them retaliate, in most cases, violently. However, the depressive effect of being a victim of school bullying doesn't wear off as the child grows.[12] Reports have shown that these effects transcend adolescence into adulthood. With so much going on, you can't afford to have your beloved kid struggling with depression alongside the responsibilities of early adulthood. So, reach out to the school to get to the bottom of the issues, and work with the school and the bully's parents to get the bully to back off.

Despite all these seemingly obvious causes of childhood depression, many parents tend to miss the most important cause of them all: themselves. Feelings are contagious, and while you think the kids are too young to comprehend what is going on with their parents, they are picking up the signals to know that Mom and/or Dad are troubled. While being a millennial parent isn't easy, do your little ones the favor of staying positive and maintaining a motivated attitude around them. This gesture will give them significantly fewer things to worry about. Spend more time self-reflecting to help you develop the right attitude toward your feelings while in your child's presence.

3. **Seek professional help as soon as possible.** When you notice changes in behavior, whether or not you identify a causing stressor, it's always important for you to seek professional help for the child. Reach out to experts who are skilled in handling wellness issues for children. They could be your child's pediatrician or a school guidance counselor.

YOUR WELLNESS RESPONSIBILITIES AS A PARENT

Kids pick up on behaviors, habits, and thought patterns. They are blank slates that get filled up really fast, and parents are responsible for most of the content that gets engraved on that precious slate of lifelong lessons. Since most of the things that they learn early follow them long into adulthood, parents need to take it upon themselves to fortify their minds with the knowledge of wellness and help kids to develop healthy habits early on in their lives. Remember the old adage, old habits die hard.

You may want to believe that your kids are too young to worry about wellness, but they are not. Your responsibility toward their budding wellness journey revolves around all eight pillars of wellness. You can help them assess their total wellness by creating a Wellness Wheel for them. This will help you figure out which areas of their lives require more attention, as well as how you can help them find a balance early enough. Your responsibilities as a parent go beyond detecting wellness challenges and fixing them. You are also required to ensure that those challenges don't occur in the first place. Or, at the very least, make sure kids don't get hit hard by life's uncertainties. There are several ways that you can do that.

While kids' physical needs are easier to detect and meet, their psychological and emotional needs require more sensitivity. Unlike providing shelter, good food, and making sure they get enough rest, to cater to your child's mental well-being, you should consider praising them for their efforts, being honest and kind to them, setting realistic goals, and encouraging them to pursue those goals. In a time of a global pandemic, socializing and playing in playgrounds and parks may not be such a safe idea to explore. Therefore, you have to take up the task of playing with your kids and encourage them to see you not only as their parent but also as their friend, who they can trust with anything. This will help keep their social skills alive throughout the pandemic until a time when the world is allowed to freely associate physically.

As parents, ensuring the safety of our children is our primary responsibility. We need to make sure that they only go out to social gatherings when it's certified safe by regulatory organizations. And even though a location is designated as safe, keep an eye on your kids to make sure they are observing personal safety protocols (which you should consider teaching them) and maintaining social distance.

You are responsible for making sure that your kids grow up in healthy and optimally stimulating environments. To do this, you can surround them with the right toys, gadgets, mentally stimulating games, books, and an environment conducive for growth. Research has shown that, regardless of parents' educational levels, kids who grew up in a house with books are more actively invested in academic and intellectual development than those that grew up in houses without books.[13]

To accomplish this, you first have to pay good attention to all areas of your well-being. It is also up to you to provide the love and emotional support that your child needs for effective development. From my experience, this can be really daunting for single parents, but it's highly achievable.

As our daily engagements become demanding, so much is required of single parents to wonder how their kids are doing. Sometimes, after an exhausting day, I wonder, how is my kid doing? How is he coping? And what can I do to help him get through the challenges that he might be facing? Most parents are filled with similar worries and concerns. And it's likely to slip through the cracks if we don't actively channel our focus toward making sure that our kids make the best out of life.

Intellectually, as well, you have to get involved in your children's lives just as much as their school teachers are. Ensuring that they engage in creative activities and stay committed to their academic activities is the responsibility of a parent—you. You need to make sure that their homework is completed on time and that their free time is well planned. You have to make sure that they are completely free to explore their creativity and reach the lengths of their mind's imaginations.

Their physical well-being isn't left out of the question. At young ages, kids lack the self-discipline to do what is right, provided they know what is (or isn't) right. So, it comes down to parents to safeguard their physical well-being. However, a lot of parents may not be doing so well in that regard. According to the Center for Disease Control and Prevention, about 14.4 million American kids and adolescents suffer from childhood obesity. While genetics and hormonal imbalance contribute minimally to this occurrence, lack of physical activities and poor eating habits are the leading causes of obesity in children.[14] You don't expect children to know how to cultivate healthy eating habits or engage in physical activities if they aren't guided into it. So, it is our responsibility, as parents, to ensure that our kids eat healthily and engage in physical activities often. Interestingly, their chances of being physically active increase when they are outgoing.

We owe kids some social responsibilities as well. You can begin teaching your children to be emotionally and socially intelligent early. They will quickly understand and begin to better influence the emotions of others, as well as themselves, as they grow and mature. It will offer them an added advantage that could put them ahead in their adult lives.

Taking your kids to parks, to sporting events, birthday parties, and encouraging them to make friends and hold conversations with other people are good ways to start laying the foundations for the social pillar of their wellness mansion. The benefits of this cannot be overstated. Socially competent kids are less likely to feel lonely, have higher self-esteem, communicate more effectively, develop faster, and experience significantly less risk of depression. Currently, however, the pandemic has created a barrier for kids to hone these social skills. Parents are worried that these important skills may be lost before the world gets back to normal. I believe that encouraging your children to exploit networking opportunities via virtual channels will be helpful.

How about finance? Are kids too young to be burdened with the power of money? Parents do not have to thrust their kids into getting jobs and earning money. However, it will be of great benefit to a child's financial future if you can teach them early enough to develop healthy financial habits like saving part of the money given to them, being accountable for how they spend their money, prioritizing expenses, and investing in the safest ways. If you have a strong business background, you can guide your kids into entrepreneurship early in their lives. With 41 percent of teenagers considering entrepreneurship as a career path, it helps for kids to learn the basics of business early in life. You can help your child get started.

Spiritually, most kids take after their parents. According to a 2020 study by the Pew Research Center, 76 percent of teenagers shared that they have the same religious beliefs as their parents. While religiosity and spirituality may not take center stage in the lives of millennials and Gen Zers, the impact on community development, cognitive growth, crime rate, and psychological wellness can't be ignored. Connecting to a purpose greater than them gives kids a foundation upon which they can build their principles, define their personal values, and carve a path for themselves. This will significantly improve their chances of happiness and self-satisfaction as adults. And you can help them start early.

▌DON'T FORGET YOURSELF

Being a parent is an amazing experience. Many of us wouldn't trade it for anything in this world. However, it can have a great effect on your well-being if you allow your wellness progress to slip through the cracks. While you focus on helping your kids develop an unshakable wellness foundation, forgetting to look after yourself could be a grave mistake. Why is that?

For one, your well-being is just as important to the kids as it is to you. Remember that kids learn more from observation than they do by just listening to you. Despite all I tell my ten-year-old son about the need for everyone to prioritize their emotional wellness by finding time to unwind and reflect, he will always call me out when I'm working too hard and neglecting or forgetting myself and my wellness. He will say, "Mom, I think you should take some time to sit down and watch TV, play some games, and get some sleep."

A lot of things are constantly demanding our attention, and it may appear to be a waste of time to stop and take some personal time, but it's totally necessary to do so. If not for your sake, do it for the kids that are watching and learning, with or without questioning.

Parenting is a tough task. Many of us juggle it with work and caring for aging parents. This can become overwhelming sooner than we think. There are times when you feel like there's too much to take in, and the glass is full. There are times when you will be in doubt. All these things are completely normal. We have limits, and that makes us human. It's also human for us to seek help when we know that we are not coping well. It's okay to speak to someone: a professional, a friend, your partner, or even a colleague. When you approach your threshold as an individual without the right coping skills and decide to deal with it alone, you can quickly spiral into depression. You don't want to have that. So, always dedicate some time amid the parenting, occupational, caregiving, and social responsibilities to reconnect with yourself.

Key Takeaways

1. Millennials make up most of the sandwich generation, pressed by the responsibilities of caring for aging parents and raising kids of their own.

2. Being an observant parent makes it easier for you to spot behavioral changes in your kid that may be early signs of anxiety and depression.

3. You have to be your children's best friend and play buddy in a time of mass lockdown. This will help them retain their ability to socialize.

4. Your well-being is important. Your kids will learn to prioritize their wellness better when they see you prioritize yours. Take them seriously, and they will take you seriously too.

CHAPTER SEVEN

Career Wellness

To restate the fact, fifty-three million millennials are in the workforce as of 2018. At 35 percent, it is the highest proportion of US workers. These millennials, who happen to make up a significant proportion of the sandwich generation, require more organization care via benefits than their predecessors. The Gen Zers, who are getting into the workforce now and growing in number, are going to demand more from organizations than any generation that has come before them. However, a majority of these demands have nothing to do with high salaries, exorbitant bonuses, or even promotions. Rather, their benefits will be centered on wellness.

It is already happening. We see the Great Resignation era following the pandemic as staff resign from their organizations to work on endeavors that are more aligned with their personal values, support their purpose, and allow them the flexibility to care for their well-being as well as those of their children and aging parents. Even though the trend persists, many of us will remain in the same shared spaces with the same traditional arrangements or more virtual-oriented ones. Wherever you may find yourself, the issues of organizational wellness persist, and while pursuing a new career may be a fascinating endeavor, the solution to the distressing nature of our various places of work is within our grasp to solve.

As technology shifts the world, a lot of us are becoming sedentary, engaging in little or no physical activities. According to the CDC, 60 percent of adult Americans do not engage in enough physical activities. This means that the majority of the country's population faces huge risks of being unfit, at least physically. The pandemic didn't make this reality any better. Now, 70 percent of white-collar staff work remotely from the comfort of their homes.[1]

While frequent commuting to a physical office can cause bouts of low-grade stress that can accumulate into really troubling conditions, commuting and everything that comes with it gives us the opportunity to get involved in physical activities. By removing daily commutes, nothing is stopping us from sitting on our chairs all day, working, and ordering whatever we need to get delivered to our doorsteps. And although we are at home, these issues are carried on the shoulders of organizations to find ways to help staff maintain total wellness. The interesting truth is that it requires more from us than it does from organizational leaders to find balance and maintain optimum wellness.

> **Career wellness** (also known as occupational wellness) is your ability to identify your purpose and choose a profession that is aligned with it. This increases your chance of working at a job that you are passionate about, enhances productivity, and reduces the chances of frustration and career-related depression.

Whether we are working remotely from home or at a physical office, work anxiety is a real issue for both staff and leaders. There is always so much work to be done, and nobody seems to be doing enough to keep the workload from becoming unbalanced. For that reason, many people are overly concerned about creeping deadlines, vaguely communicated expectations by bosses and colleagues, and even the pressure of not wanting to fail at what we do. Amid all of these stressors, more than half of millennials are still trying to figure their lives out.[2] It's mind blowing.

I won't fail to mention the confusion that plagues many people trying to navigate their professional careers. Organizations are more diverse than they have ever been, with a mix of members from vastly different socioeconomic, cultural, religious, and ethnic backgrounds. Yet these organizations are cutting off middle-management jobs, making vertical growth in organizations more competitive and distressing.[3] Considering the fact that many millennials have pursued MBAs and other related degrees that were intended to help them start their career in higher-level management positions, there is a growing number of confused people out there who are barely living up to their professional potential.

All of these rapid changes in the corporate world have affected the lives of many and the environment. It has aggravated the stress level in society and caused many people to become disengaged from organizational activities. These are the primary causes of the wide-ranging depression that fills shared spaces today. But how can we help improve these situations? What can be done better? What individual roles can we play to help nurture organizations where the well-being of everyone is not just written in policies but put into daily practice?

REMEMBER YOUR CHORES

Recall in chapter four, where we discussed how we alone are responsible for our wellness rather than the organizations that we work with are. This doesn't negate the fact that organizations also have a role to play. And some of the leading organizations are playing those roles really well. However, the question that everyone should ask themselves is: are you playing your role well? Are you doing your wellness chores?

Because if you are not, it doesn't matter what an organization is offering you. You will find yourself struggling with anxiety over personal issues that are passing through the work-life filter. The huge health benefits, paid healthy meals, sophisticated gym membership, unlimited vacation, and all of those great perks—none of them will matter. You owe yourself the duty of finding balance in your life by identifying your values, building a life principle, and discovering your purpose.

Great organizations are characterized by great leaders that can spot your strengths and weaknesses from a mile away. The best leaders know how to harness the strengths of the organization's staff while shifting the focus away from their weaknesses. Nevertheless, these leaders are not always 100 percent accurate with their assumptions of your strengths. They can't know you as well as you can get to know yourself. Blocking out the time to reflect and discover your strongest natural assets will help you position yourself properly for opportunities in any organization in which you find yourself.

Nevertheless, even if you are in sync with your being (body and mind), there are still struggles in shared spaces that you must cultivate the wisdom to handle. Some may come from your colleagues, others from your bosses, but many will come from within. In this chapter, I will address some of the challenges that are typically found in organizations and offer solutions to help.

ORGANIZATIONAL BULLYING, RACISM, AND OTHER MISCONDUCT

Several big organizations have been accused of bullying and organizational misconduct that has had a huge impact on the wellness of their staff. In simple terms, bullying within an organization is when staff members are treated disrespectfully and unfairly, especially by a superior staff member or boss, as the case may be. In 2019, more than 90 percent of American adults reported that they had been bullied at work.[4] This is very sobering, considering that we spend more than one-third of our time in the organizations where these behaviors happen.

Working at these organizations can be a terrible experience if you're dealing with bullying by a colleague or boss. When the bullying comes from colleagues, the offender may see it as harmless jokes, but to the person being bullied, it is far more serious than that. Bullying can result in severe shock, vulnerability, and anger, especially if false information has been spread about you. In the case of a boss making harsh remarks and unconstructive criticism about your efforts, loss of confidence, frustration, helplessness, and loss of concentration can become real battles.

The effect that bullying has on the organization is just as unpleasant. People are less willing to work with a boss or in an organization where their self-esteem and egos are constantly bruised. The morale of the team takes a hit, and so does productivity. Organizations spend more money and time on work that could have happened faster if not for this downness in spirit. Consequently, when things are not moving forward as well as they should, people get stressed and easily agitated. But organizations spend large sums of money on wellness initiatives in the bid to help their staff become better, don't they?

Bullying and other organizational misconduct can hinder the progress of the wellness programs that organizations are investing in. No matter how much you talk about a healthy work environment and the staff members' responsibility to themselves as regards wellness, organizations might be washing money and efforts down the drain if they do not address the issues of bullying, racism, and other misconduct, including discrimination.

At times, the affected individuals have no intention of negatively impacting the organization's productivity. In most cases, bullying, racial slurs, and other misconduct are reactions to events happening in their personal lives. However, if we can do better by monitoring how we feel inside, as well as acknowledging how our comments and actions affect the emotions of others around us, organizational misconduct will be minimized. So, what can you do on your part to reduce the occurrence of this harsh behavior at the organization where you work?

Express your displeasure (or other emotions) in a healthy way. Knowing that some people do not really know that they themselves are bullies is one reason to do this. Respectfully telling them that their behavior is unacceptable to you and suggesting that they stop doing it can help bring their awareness to the problem. However, expressing your displeasure to bullies sometimes makes them feel like you are standing up to them. And bullies are rarely comfortable with confrontation. The outcome of your expression in this case may not be as expected. Therefore, it would be prudent of you to speak with someone that you trust within the organization and have them join you in addressing the bully. In this way, the bully will be discouraged from taking any further hostile actions.

Journaling is also helpful in dealing with organizational misconduct. Keeping a record of the time when an incident occurred, as well as the date, nature of events, witnesses present, and the outcome of the encounter can help you establish a pattern of behavior. This will help you understand a person better. Sometimes people act harshly, and it's not because they don't like you or because they enjoy bullying others. Sometimes they could be dealing with something in their personal lives and are only reacting because they can't contain it any longer. Keeping a clear journal of people's behaviors, especially someone that's bullying you, can improve your observation of that person. Maybe you can help them get through what they're dealing with. Who knows? We all need someone in our corner that cares at some point, don't we?

You should report incidents to superior staff or senior management. It may be out of place or uncomfortable telling colleagues how to behave in a shared space. However, a superior is the right person to make or suggest behavioral corrections. So, when someone repeatedly acts in a manner that is condescending toward you, or acts unprofessionally, it is a best practice for you to reach out to your boss or supervisor and lodge a formal complaint. There are organizations where subtle bullying is a part of the fabric, and reporting to a superior could result in making you look weaker. Speaking up respectfully, in that case, might be a good option to consider. Nevertheless, if your team considers bullying behaviors to be the norm, then your boss or supervisor must have condoned it for a while. In some cases, they may be the ones passing the behavior down to you and other staff members. Reporting to that person may not make a lot of difference. Instead, you can send a report to senior management with an articulate breakdown of the offending behavior as recorded in your journal. This will bring the person's behavioral pattern to management's attention and could possibly positively influence organizational policies.

However, no matter what happens, never retaliate. Retaliation only leads to violence. When you retaliate, it could confuse management because they may not be able to decipher who the perpetrator really is, because both you and the offender/bully are disregarding the organization's code of conduct. When violence is a violation of an organization's policies, you may be on the receiving end of disciplinary actions. You should make sure to avoid this. Healthily expressing your disapproval of the behavior and reporting to superiors if the behavior persists are the most sensible steps to follow.

YOUR WELL-BEING DURING A JOB AND CAREER TRANSITION

Changing jobs and careers can be stressful. There are new people to meet, new protocols to learn and follow, new skills to develop, a new environment to adapt to, if not remote, and likely a new vision or mission to adopt and pursue. However, this stress is not stopping people from making up to seven career changes throughout their lifetime. But I'm sure you can guess how draining changing careers is to their well-being.

A lot of people frown at the idea of changing jobs or careers because of the enormous amount of stress that comes with it. A few persons may have to face this grueling experience in search of a career that best suits their personal values and beliefs. Some of the reasons why many people don't consider a change in job or career are closely linked to the effects on their wellness. Nevertheless, if you follow the steps described in this book, you will realize that it's much easier than you could imagine to find a job or career that offers true satisfaction.

Many people focus too much on their weaknesses, so they are constantly searching for work in an organization where they fit. Interestingly enough, they could fit anywhere if only they could focus on their strengths and worry less about what they believe they are not good at. By spending some quiet time alone, self-reflecting, you will draw closer to finding what your true strengths are and discover how you can use those newly discovered strengths to make your current job more satisfactory.

Signs to Look out for before Changing Jobs or Careers

- Dreading the work you do (hating Mondays)
- Being grossly unhappy with your choice of profession
- Being always buried in work, without support from colleagues and consideration from managers
- Having growth stunted no matter how hard you try
- Feeling left out or out of place, even when colleagues try to carry you along

---

An important part of finding fulfillment in our work is being clear in knowing what we want. You could change careers many times and still not find the satisfaction that you seek. You would simply move around with the same problem from one job to another. It's true that many of us want a healthy work-life balance.[5] However, the idea of this balance is unrealistic to most. Consider that folks want better pay and healthier benefits like paid sick leave, paid unlimited vacation, maternity leave for male staff members, and other perks. It may not be a very good idea for organizations to pay staff a hefty sum for them to spend less time at work under the guise of work-life balance. This has spurred some of the rapid changes in jobs and careers today.

Nevertheless, a better work-life balance may be an endless search without identifying what you really want from your life and work. So, taking some time to identify your values, principles, and beliefs can help you navigate a major career change. There's nothing better than working on something you believe in and having that strongly aligned with your personal values. Every day, you will find out that working only makes your life more balanced. Imagine a job that allows you to go forest bathing as a nature lover. Or a career where your love for numbers never ends. Or a wildlife conservation project in East Africa for someone whose belief rests on the protection of nature and the environment.

Not everyone will get to work in organizations that outright support their values, principles, and beliefs. Some of us may find ourselves working in companies that do not align with our personalities or interests, just to make ends meet. But for what it's worth, you can find a way to connect your personal beliefs with your work in a way that you enjoy enormously. President John F. Kennedy once met a janitor at NASA that said he was "helping put a man on the moon."

Although the janitor was not a rocket scientist, he believed in space exploration and understood his role as a part of the Apollo mission, understanding that without the janitors keeping the premises clean and hygienic for the scientists, their work would be even more difficult.

While changing careers may seem fun for those seeking a new adventure, many don't really give it deep thought. Many people focus on themselves when making a career transition. They are concerned about how much money they can make, what the benefits are, or the kind of office they will be working from and the people they will be working with. These perks can only appear fun for as long as they are new. Sooner or later, you will get accustomed to them, the newness will wear off, and that will suck the fun out of everything. Focusing solely on yourself makes working at a new organization more stressful. Also, when you are not the best in the company, it stirs up insecurity and a constant need to prove a point.

So, instead of focusing on what you could stand to benefit from a new job, instead think about what you will be doing for others. Whom do you want to serve? How can you serve them best, and how will serving them make their lives better? These are the questions you should be answering every time you want to make a career choice. When you are serving the people you really want to serve, you will not be worked up about how terrible you may be at the job because, with every happy customer or client, your job satisfaction will reach a new high. It doesn't matter what company you work for or what position you hold; you should tie your job satisfaction to how you make other people better. You will have yourself to thank for that.

Tips to Improve Your Career Wellness

- Straighten out your priorities.
- Be growth-oriented by focusing on creating more value.
- Find a balance between life and work.
- Commit some time to engage in recreations and hobbies.

As you build a sturdy career or attempt to by exploring other options, don't forget to be mindful of your financial well-being. Money-related stressors can push you into making irrational career decisions. What's more interesting is that even though you may get a job that pays better, making more money brings considerably higher stress and, in most cases, could affect your productivity at work.[6] And that won't really stop you from worrying about student loans, emergency expenses, or credit card debts. These financial stressors will follow you regardless of career choice. So, it's really up to you to make sure you don't have them in the first place.

To avoid financial stressors from negatively influencing your decisions when making major career changes, you have to start saving. It's better to start early, but it's never too late to start now. Actively learn about money and how it works. This will bring to your attention how many of the expenses that you thought really matter don't matter so much. Also, put together an emergency fund to shoulder unforeseen expenses in the event that you experience financial trouble or are unable to work. This can help save you from mounting credit card debt. By using this strategy, you can pursue more adventures in your career with a clearer mind, knowing that you are not making major life and career decisions under duress.

Key Takeaways

1. Many of us are living a sedentary lifestyle, working from home through virtual spaces, and not engaging in enough physical activity.

2. You should identify and attend to your wellness responsibilities because your organization is limited in what it can do. Find your strengths and use them to improve your chances for career growth.

3. Many people (90 percent) experience organizational misconduct, including bullying, racism, or other forms of discrimination.

4. Not everyone may work at their dream organization, but you can turn your current career into a dream career by aligning your personal beliefs, principles, and strengths with the values of the organization that you work for.

Endnotes

Introduction: The Generational Wellness Gap

1. LJ Miller and W Lu (2018). "Gen Z Is Set to Outnumber Millennials Within a Year." *Bloomberg.* <https://www.bloomberg.com/news/articles/2018-08-20/gen-z-to-outnumber-millennials-within-a-year-demographic-trends>

2. R Fry (2018). "Millennials are the largest generation in the U.S. labor force." Pew Research Center. <https://www.pewresearch.org/fact-tank/2018/04/11/millennials-largest-generation-us-labor-force/>

3. BCBS Association (2019). "The Health of Millennials." <https://www.bcbs.com/the-health-of-america/reports/the-health-of-millennials>

4. JM Twenge, AB Cooper, TE Joiner, ME Duffy and SG Binau (2019). "Age, Period, and Cohort Trends in Mood Disorder Indicators and Suicide-Related Outcomes in a Nationally Representative Dataset, 2005–2017." *Journal of Abnormal Psychology*, 128(3), 185–199. <http://dx.doi.org/10.1037/abn0000410>

Chapter One: The Wellness You Never Knew

1. H Frisch, G Granditsch, and E Wurst (1979). "Psychosomal dwarfism with reversible growth hormone deficiency." *Wiener klinische Wochenschrift.*

2. A Lischka, C Groh, H Frisch, M T Schubert, and E Tatzer (1984). "Psychosocial dwarfism—a rare form of growth disorder." *Wiener klinische Wochenschrift*.

3. Various authors (2020). "Defining The Mental Wellness Economy." Global Wellness Institute.

4. H Elliott (2021). "Naomi Osaka withdraws from Wimbledon, plans to compete in Olympics; Nadal skips both." *Los Angeles Times*.

5. S Pandey (2021). "What are twisties that caused Simone Biles to withdraw from gymnastics events?" *First Post*.

6. Various authors (2020). "How Many Americans Have Lost Jobs with Employer Health Coverage During the Pandemic?" CommonWealth Fund.

7. D Ding, BP Cruz, MA Green, and AE Bauman (2020). "Is the COVID-19 lockdown nudging people to be more active: a big data analysis." *British Journal of Sports Medicine*.

8. A McKee (2017). "A 3-Step Process to Break a Cycle of Frustration, Stress, and Fighting at Work." *Harvard Business Review*.

9. Various authors (2018). "'Training' your mind to improve well-being." Harvard University T.H. Chan School of Public Health.

10. Dr. J Castleberry (2020). "Determination and Leadership Part 2: Purpose, Planning, and Persistence." *President's Blog*, Northwestern University. <https://www.northwestu. edu/president/blog/determination-and-leadership-part-2-purpose-planning-and-persistence>

11. Various authors (2011). "Angelina Jolie sells Winston Churchill painting for record £7m." BBC.

12. M Hilburn-Arnold (2020). "Turning to Creativity: A Grounded Theory Approach Towards Understanding the

Relationship Between Wellness and the Arts for Adolescents."
University of Texas at San Antonio.

13. TS Conner, CG DeYoung, and PJ Silvia (2016). "Everyday creative activity as a path to flourishing." *The Journal of Positive Psychology*.

14. L Vermeer, A Muth, D Terenzi, and SQ Park (2021). "Curiosity for information predicts well-being during COVID-19 Pandemic: Contributions of loneliness and daily lifestyle." German Institute of Human Nutrition.

15. TB Kashdan, P Rose, and FD Fincham (2010). "Curiosity and Exploration: Facilitating Positive Subjective Experiences and Personal Growth Opportunities." *Journal of Personal Assessment*.

16. Dr. E Hoffman (2021). "Curiosity: A Key to wellbeing." White Swan Foundation. <https://www.whiteswanfoundation.org/mental-health-matters/wellbeing/curiosity-a-key-to-wellbeing>

Chapter Two: The 8 Pillars of Wellness

1. JJ Gross and RW Levenson (1997). "Hiding feelings: The acute effects of inhibiting negative and positive emotion." *Journal of Abnormal Psychology*, 106(1).

2. A Gallo (2012). "How to Work with Someone You Hate." *Harvard Business Review*.

3. T Zorn and KW Gregory (2005). "Learning the Ropes Together: Assimilation and Friendship Development Among First-Year Male Medical Students." *Journal of Health Communication*, 17(3).

4. D Stephan (2019). "Ways to Raise Money: The Ultimate Guide to Raising Startup Capital." *Crunchbase*. <https://about.crunchbase.com/blog/raising-startup-capital/>

5. Various authors (2016). "Evidence for Social Wellness - Part 1." American Counseling Association. <https://www.nih.gov/health-information/social-wellness-toolkit>

6. Various authors (2016). "Relationships in the 21st Century." Mental Health Foundation.

7. DZ Levin, J Walter, and JK Murnighan (2017). "Dormant Ties: The Value Of Reconnecting." Academy of Management Proceedings.

8. S Wingate (2019). "Brazilian Couple Spends 20 Years Planting Millions Of Trees On A Barren Cattle Ranch To Create A 1,750-Acre Paradise For Animals Pushed Out By Deforestation." *The Daily Mail* (UK).

9. SH Eickmann, AC Lima, MQ Guerra, MC Lima, PI Lira, SR Huttly, and A Ashworth (2003). "Improved cognitive and motor development in a community-based intervention of psychosocial stimulation in northeast Brazil." *Developmental Medicine and Child Neurology Journal*, 45(8).

10. A Shashkevich (2018). "Stanford Scholar Tackles The History Of People's Obsession With Crystals." Stanford University Press Office.

11. Various authors. "Environmental Wellness." Northwestern University, Washington DC.

12. MB Cannon (2013). "Exploring the Nature of Space for Human Behavior in Ordinary Structured Environments." University of Nebraska – Lincoln.

13. C Martin and M Dent (2019). "How Nestle, Google And Other Businesses Make Money By Going Green." *Los Angeles Times*.

14. Z Ingilizian, M Ghosh, and B Bovis (2021). "Reusing 10% will stop almost half of plastic waste from entering the ocean. Here's how." World Economic Forum.

15. Various authors (2015). "Religious Composition by Country, 2010-2050." Pew Research Center.

16. Various authors (2006). "The impact of spirituality on mental health." Mental Health Foundation.

17. R Bonelli, RE Dew, HG Koenig, DH Rosmarin, and S Vasegh (2012). "Religious and spiritual factors in depression: review and integration of the research." *Depression Research and Treatment Journal*.

18. Various authors (2016). "Religion in Everyday Life." Pew Research Center.

19. B Johnson, D Larson, S Li, and SJ Jang (2000). "Escaping from the Crime of Inner Cities: Church Attendance and Religious Salience among Disadvantaged Youth." *Justice Quarterly*, 17.

20. C Vieten et al. (2018). "Future directions in meditation research: Recommendations for expanding the field of contemplative science." *PLOS One*.

21. MR Chowdhury (2021). "5 Health Benefits of Daily Meditation According to Science." *Positive Psychology*. <https://positivepsychology.com/benefits-of-meditation/>

22. N Johannes, M Vuorre, and AK Przybylski (2021). "Video game play is positively correlated with well-being." *Royal Society Open Science*.

23. JC Rosser Jr, PJ Lynch, L Cuddihy, DA Gentile, J Klonsky, R Merrell (2007). "The impact of video games on training surgeons in the 21st century." *The Archives of Surgery*.

24. Various authors (2016). "The State of American Jobs: How Americans view their jobs." Pew Research Center.

25. J Clifton (2017). "The World's Broken Workplace." Gallup.

26. M Leonhardt (2021). "61% of older millennials believe they'll be working at least part-time during retirement." CNBC.

Chapter Three: The Wellness Wheel

1. MJ de la Merced (2021). "'It went to my head': Adam Neumann has regrets about his time at WeWork." *New York Times*.

Chapter Four: Sharing the Chores

1. K Elkins (2017). "A brief history of the 401(k), which changed how Americans retire." CNBC.

2. DG Passey, K Hammerback, A Huff, JR Harris, and PA Hannon (2018). "The Role of Managers in Employee Wellness Programs: A Mixed-Methods Study." *American Journal of Health Promotion*, 32(8), 1697–1705.

3. A Di Crosta et al. (2021). "Psychological factors and consumer behavior during the COVID-19 pandemic." *PLOS One*.

4. F Richter (2021). "COVID-19 has caused a huge amount of lost working hours." World Economic Forum.

5. Various authors (2021). "Lockdown weight gain averaging half a stone - survey." BBC

6. AL Lin, E Vittinghoff, JE Olgin, MJ Pletcher, and GM Marcus (2021). "Body Weight Changes During Pandemic-Related Shelter-in-Place in a Longitudinal Cohort Study." *JAMA Network Open*, 4(3).

7. R Brand, S Timme, and S Nosrat (2020). "When Pandemic Hits: Exercise Frequency and Subjective Well-Being During COVID-19 Pandemic." *Frontiers in Psychology*, 11(0).

8. E Gorgenyi-Hegyes, RJ Nathan, and M Fekete-Farkas (2021). "Workplace Health Promotion, Employee Wellbeing and Loyalty during Covid-19 Pandemic—Large Scale Empirical Evidence from Hungary." *Economies*, 9.

9. Various authors (2020). "Four Types of Suicides." Management Development Institute of Singapore. <https://www.mdis.edu.sg/blog/four-types-of-suicides/>

10. A Alimujiang et al. (2019). "Association Between Life Purpose and Mortality Among US Adults Older Than 50 Years." *JAMA Network Open*, 2(5).

11. R Woolworth (2019). "Great Mentors Focus on the Whole Person, Not Just Their Career." *Harvard Business Review*.

12. Various authors (retrieved Nov. 2021). "Health Risks of Secondhand Smoke." American Cancer Society. <https://www.cancer.org/healthy/stay-away-from-tobacco/health-risks-of-tobacco/secondhand-smoke.html>

13. N Christakis, J Fowler (2009). *Connected* (New York: Little, Brown, and Company).

14. J Helliwell, R Putnam (2005). "The social context of well-being." Cited in F Huppert, N Baylis, B Keverne (Eds.), *The Science of Well-Being* (Oxford: Oxford University Press).

Chapter Five: 5 Steps to Complete Wellness

1. G Knell, CP Durand, HW Kohl, IHC Wu, Gabriel K Pettee (2019). "Prevalence and Likelihood of Meeting Sleep, Physical Activity, and Screen-Time Guidelines Among US Youth." *JAMA Pediatrics*, 173(4).

2. M Hanson (2021). "Student Loan Debt by Generation." Education Data Initiative. <https://educationdata.org/student-loan-debt-by-generation>

3. R Siegel and T Telford (2019). "More work, more sleep: New study offers glimpse of daily life as a millennial." *The Washington Post*.

4. T Eurich (2018). "What Self-Awareness Really Is (and How to Cultivate It)." *Harvard Business Review.*

5. Various authors (2019). "Critical Thinking Versus Problem Solving." Drexel University Goodwin College of Professional Studies. <https://drexel.edu/graduatecollege/professional-development/blog/2019/october/critical-thinking-versus-problem-solving/>

6. AJ Cairns et al. (2019). "Goal setting improves retention in youth mental health: a cross-sectional analysis." *Child and Adolescent Psychiatry and Mental Health Journal*, 13, 31.

7. AJ Elliot and HA McGregor (2001). "A 2 × 2 achievement goal framework." *Journal of Personality and Social Psychology*, 80(3).

8. GT Doran (1981). "There's a S.M.A.R.T. way to write management's goals and objectives." *Management Review*, 70 (11).

9. SG Cook (2013). "Use Your Personal Strengths for Success, Wellbeing." *Women in Higher Education*, 22(3), 20-21

10. G Cipollone et al. (2020). "Exploring the Role of Caffeine Use in Adult-ADHD Symptom Severity of US Army Soldiers." *Journal of Clinical Medicine*, 9(11).

11. SJ Lepore, HJ Miles, and JS Levy (1997). "Relation of Chronic and Episodic Stressors to Psychological Distress, Reactivity, and Health Problems." *International Journal of Behavioral Medicine*, 4, 39-59.

12. KM Korpela, M Ylén, L Tyrväinen, and H Silvennoinen (2008). "Determinants of Restorative Experiences in Everyday Favorite Places." *Health & Place*, 14.

13. ES Morita et al. (2007). "Psychological Effects of Forest Environments on Healthy Adults: Shinrin-Yoku (Forest-Air

Bathing, Walking) As a Possible Method of Stress Reduction." *Public Health*, 121.

14. L Landry (2019). "Why Emotional Intelligence Is Important In Leadership." *Harvard Business School Online*. <https://online. hbs.edu/blog/post/emotional-intelligence-in-leadership>

15. Daniel Goleman (2004). "What Makes a Leader?" *Harvard Business Review*.

Chapter Six: Parental Wellness

1. K Steinmetz (2020). "My Parents Are Millennials." *TIME*.

2. Various authors (2020). "What is the U.S. Opioid Epidemic?" United States Department of Health and Human Services.

3. Various authors (2021). "Millennial Parents: What Makes Them So Different?" *Times of India*.

4. Various authors (2020). "Taking Care of Your Parents: Exploring Millennials' Plan to Care for Their Aging Parents." CaringAdvisor. <https://caringadvisor.com/ taking-care-of-your-parents/>

5. H Hoffower (2019). "Meet the average American millennial, who has an $8,000 net worth, is delaying life milestones because of student loan debt, and still relies on their parents for money." *Business Insider*.

6. K Parker and E Patten (2013). "The Sandwich Generation." Pew Research Center.

7. P Klass, M.D. (2021). "How to Spot Depression in Young Children." *New York Times*.

8. D Becker (2021). "'We Can Talk About This': Kids Benefit When Parents Open Up About Mental Health Struggles." WBUR-FM.

9. RS Diler, WB Daviss, A Lopez, D Axelson, S Iyengar, and B Birmaher (2007). "Differentiating major depressive disorder in youths with attention deficit hyperactivity disorder." *Journal of Affective Disorders*, 102(1-3), 125-130.

10. RL Coley and M Kull (2019). "Is Moving During Childhood Harmful?" The MacArthur Foundation.

11. AS Bergman, U Axberg, E Hanson (2017). "When a parent dies – a systematic review of the effects of support programs for parentally bereaved children and their caregivers." *BMC Palliative Care*, 16, 39.

12. R Kaltiala-Heino and S Fröjd (2011). "Correlation between bullying and clinical depression in adolescent patients." *Adolescent Health, Medicine and Therapeutics Journal*, 2, 37–44.

13. MDR Evans et al. (2010). "Family Scholarly Culture and Educational Success: Books and schooling in 27 nations." *Research in Social Stratification and Mobility Journal*, 28(2), 171–197.

14. CG Fairburn and KD Brownell (Ed.) (2005). *Eating Disorders and Obesity: A Comprehensive Handbook* (Guilford Press).

Chapter Seven: Career Wellness

1. L Saad And JM Jones (2021). "Seven In 10 U.S. White-Collar Workers Still Working Remotely." Gallup.

2. J Liu (2021). "Almost half of older millennials wish they'd chosen a different career path—what they'd do differently." CNBC.

3. G Anders (2008). "Overseeing More Employees With Fewer Managers." *Wall Street Journal*.

4. M Backman (2019). "More than 90% of employees say they've been bullied at work." *USA Today*.

5. F Alesso-Bendisch (2020). "Millennials Want A Healthy Work-Life Balance. Here's What Bosses Can Do." *Forbes*.

6. B Pinsker (2016). "Money stress is a productivity killer at work." Reuters.

Author Bio

As Founding Partner of Glymph Consulting, LLC., a consulting firm that focuses on business infrastructure development and mentoring, as well as individual wellness, Rikimah Glymph is a writer, mentor, and advocate for equal rights and opportunity. With over a decade of experience affecting change in both the political and civil worlds, Rikimah has served as the Chief of People & State Operations for Bernie 2020 and as the Global Director of People Operations for Dimagi. Rikimah has a B.A. in History, an MBA, and a Master's in Project Management—but, most importantly, she has a passion for improving the lives of those around her.

While her experiences have positioned her to have in-depth knowledge and firsthand understanding of what others might need, Rikimah's heart is what led her to write *Total Wellness*. She knows all too well the everyday challenges younger generations face growing up in a rapidly changing world, and she strives to improve their well-being with this book. She hopes it will challenge them to think outside of their comfort zones and to help them create innovative solutions necessary for change.

Made in the USA
Middletown, DE
01 April 2025

73601118R00118